**Also by the Authors**

Been There Got Out: Toxic Relationships,
High Conflict Divorce, And How To Stay Sane
Under Insane Circumstances

**BEEN THERE GOT OUT**

# WHEN YOUR EX TURNS THE KIDS AGAINST YOU

BEEN THERE GOT OUT

# WHEN YOUR EX TURNS THE KIDS AGAINST YOU

Lisa Johnson & Chris Barry
Forward by Bill Eddy, LCSW, Esq.

where words connect

This is a work of nonfiction.
Been There Got Out: When Your Ex Turns the Kids Against You

All rights are reserved. No part of this book may be used or reproduced in any manner without the copyright owner's written permission, except for quotations in book reviews.

Copyright © 2025 Lisa Johnson and Chris Barry

ISBN: 978-1-967674-18-3 (Paperback)
ISBN: 978-1-967674-19-0 (eBook)
Library of Congress Control Number: 2025927273

1st Edition

Authors' pictures Photographer credit: Ana Szilagyi
Print and eBook Layout Design: Amit Dey
Cover Design: Okomato
Editor: Winsome Hudson

Website: www.wordeee.com
Twitter.com/wordeeeupdates
Facebook: facebook.com/Wordeee/
e-mail: contact@wordeee.com
Published by Wordeee in the United States, New York, New York 2025
Printed in the USA

# DISCLAIMER

This book does not contain legal, financial, or mental health advice. The opinions expressed in this publication are those of the authors. The information in this book is intended to furnish readers with general information on matters they may find to be of interest. The information contained herein is provided for general guidance and is not intended to replace or substitute for professional legal advice, consultation, or service.

All quotes attributed to our coaching clients are actual quotes. Names of clients have been changed to protect anonymity.

In the event of immediate domestic abuse or danger, call 911. For anonymous, confidential help in the United States, call the National Domestic Violence Hotline at 800-799-7233.

# DEDICATION

To our clients, and to those out there who are suffering and don't even know what they're dealing with...yet.

# ADVANCE PRAISE

"When Your Ex Turns The Kids Against You is a must-have guide on how to recognize parental alienation, the ways it affects you and your family, plus steps for navigating the legal system to protect you and your children. I applaud Lisa and Chris for raising awareness about this poorly understood subject and for providing practical and invaluable guidance. Every parent should have a copy of this excellent book."

—*Charlie McCready,*
*Parental Alienation Coach*

"If you've been living a nightmare like the title of this book, know that you're not alone. Lisa Johnson and Chris Barry have "been there and gotten out" and can be your wise, gentle guides through this incredibly challenging time."

—*Dr. Christopher Willard,*
*Psychologist, Author, and Harvard Psychiatry Professor*

"As someone who has both lived through this and counseled others, I know firsthand how invaluable Lisa and Chris' guidance is. *When Your Ex Turns the Kids Against You* proves that knowledge is your superpower, offering compassionate, practical steps to protect yourself while navigating the pain of high-conflict divorce. This book has the power to save years of heartache, both personally and professionally."

—*Jessica Anne Pressler, LCSW*

"This book is such a practical guide for one of the hardest parenting challenges—when your child starts pulling away because of an ex's influence. Lisa & Chris take a painful, confusing experience and give you clear, step-by-step strategies to handle it. What I love most is that it's not just theory or sympathy; it's actual tools you can use right now. The book helps you know what to say, how to respond, and how to keep your relationship with your kids strong, even in a high-conflict co-parenting situation. If you're dealing with parental alienation, this book is a lifeline."

—*Darlynn Childress, Parent Coach*
*Host*, Become A Calm Mama *Podcast*

"Lisa and Chris have written another wonderful resource for parents going through a contentious divorce. They not only provide useful, practical tips for navigating the legal world of high-conflict divorce and custody battles, but also important guidance on how to navigate the challenging emotional situations that arise, with a keen focus on children's emotional and developmental needs. With sensitivity and compassion, they provide guidance for parents on how to manage their own (understandable) reactions to best support their children (and ultimately themselves)."

—*Jill Leibowitz, Psy.D., Clinical Psychologist*
*Author, The Untold Story of Itsy Bitsy Children's Book Series*

"As someone who works closely with children and families navigating high-conflict divorce, I see every day how devastating parental alienation can be. *Been There Got Out: When Your Ex Turns the Kids Against You* offers clear, compassionate, and practical guidance that validates parents' experiences while centering the well-being of children. This book is an invaluable resource for families, professionals, and anyone seeking to understand and interrupt the cycle of alienation."

—*Adam Barta, LCSW-R, PC,*
*Head In The Right Direction Counseling Services*

"This book is an important resource for anyone seeking to understand parental alienation in high-conflict custody dynamics. It breaks down the emotional and legal challenges families often face, offering insights that are both compassionate and deeply informative. A valuable contribution to the conversation, it sheds light on a controversial topic that deserves far more awareness and understanding."

—*Tyra Juliette Schwartz,*
*Author, The Sky is Red*

"A vital, compassionate, and eye-opening guide that reveals how children are shaped by parental conflict. It offers the insight and tools needed to protect their emotional well-being."

—*Theresa Inman,*
*Board-Certified Behavior Analyst*

"One of the greatest, often unspoken personal travesties of our time is when one parent alienates the other parent from their child's life, either overtly or covertly, whether doing so emotionally, physically, or through weaponizing the court system. Lisa and Chris speak directly to this issue in ways that are helpful and enlightening to all who read. Their passion to help those who are enduring narcissistic abuse comes through in their new book, offering practical advice and solutions for those who are enduring it - all the while making it a fantastic resource for those who provide comfort and care for parents enduring this hardship. Their voice is so very needed in our world, and this book is so very welcome where victims of this abuse in our culture go largely unknown and unnoticed."

—*Jon McKenney, Coach and Author*

"Consider this essential reading for any parent who feels their children are turning away from them. The holistic lens that Lisa and Chris take in this book—addressing the legal system, behaviors of the other parent, and the feelings of the children themselves—is critical in gaining an understanding of the complexity of this issue. The practical tools and strategies are straightforward and instrumental to preserving any parent's relationship with their child."

—*AJ Gajjar,*
*Child Development Specialist,*
*Parenting and Trauma Consultant*

# TABLE OF CONTENTS

Foreword . . . . . . . . . . . . . . . . . . . . . . . . . . . . . . . . . . . . . . . . xvii

Introduction . . . . . . . . . . . . . . . . . . . . . . . . . . . . . . . . . . . . . . xx

Chapter 1: Alienation vs. Estrangement . . . . . . . . . . . . . . . . . . . . . . 1

Chapter 2: The Impact of Alienation . . . . . . . . . . . . . . . . . . . . . . . 15

Chapter 3: A Distorted View of Reality: Why They Do It . . . . . . . 38

Chapter 4: How It Begins: Pre-Alienation and Poisonous Messages . . . . . . . . . . . . . . . . . . . . . . . . . . . . . . . . . . . 45

Chapter 5: The Tentacles of Poison . . . . . . . . . . . . . . . . . . . . . . . . 60

Chapter 6: Oh. My. God. (What Can I DO?) . . . . . . . . . . . . . . . . . . 77

Chapter 7: Getting Yourself Right . . . . . . . . . . . . . . . . . . . . . . . . . 87

Chapter 8: Gearing Up for A(nother) Legal Battle . . . . . . . . . . . . 101

Chapter 9: Building Your Team: Choosing the Right Professionals . . . . . . . . . . . . . . . . . . . . . . . . . . . . . . 119

Chapter 10: Nailing Your Presentation . . . . . . . . . . . . . . . . . . . . . 139

Chapter 11: Parenting Plans, Relief, & Enforcement . . . . . . . . . . . 153

Chapter 12: What's Most Important: Creating Stability for Your Kids . . . . . . . . . . . . . . . . . . . . . . . . . . . . . . . . . 165

Chapter 13: Understanding What's Going On Inside Them:
    Interacting with Your Children. . . . . . . . . . . . . . . . . . 177

Chapter 14: When Anger Becomes Aggression. . . . . . . . . . . . . . 188

Chapter 15: Dealing with the Devil. . . . . . . . . . . . . . . . . . . . . . . . 207

Chapter 16: Staying Strong & Seeing it Through. . . . . . . . . . . . . 216

Acknowledgements . . . . . . . . . . . . . . . . . . . . . . . . . . . . . . . . . . . 221

About the Authors . . . . . . . . . . . . . . . . . . . . . . . . . . . . . . . . . . . 223

# FOREWORD

When I first connected with Lisa Johnson and Chris Barry about a year ago, I was very pleased to hear about their good work with parents dealing with alienated children. While they are not officially professionals in the field of family law and family counseling, they have come up from the trenches and become expert coaches and educators instead. Based on their own divorce experiences, they can truly empathize with what parents are going through. But they have also done a lot of learning and research on what is really going on in this traumatic area of family life. The result is their ongoing work with individual parents and this powerful, sensitive, and highly informative book, *Been There Got Out: When Your Ex Turns the Kids Against You.*

As a family lawyer and therapist, I want to give you two key points for some additional context as you read this book. First, as a lawyer, I am glad that they mention "estrangement," which is the term most often used when a child rejects a parent because of that parent's own behavior (such as child abuse, domestic violence, or overwhelmingly emotional parenting).

I have handled many cases in and out of court where such abuse is occurring. In most of these cases, children do not reject either parent. On the other hand, "alienation" is the term commonly used when a child resists contact with one parent because of what the other parent ("favored parent") says and does in relation to the "rejected parent." Both abuse and alienation are real and serious family problems.

As you will read, this book is specifically about alienation and not about estrangement. But you should be aware that there are some people who deny that alienation exists, saying it is "junk science" and that there is no legitimate research on this subject. This is absolutely false. They say this because some parents and children have been harmed when true abuse has been disregarded as alienation. However, based on my three decades of experience with this subject as a lawyer, most professionals today (lawyers, therapists, judges, and mediators) agree that there is such a thing as "alienating behaviors" and there is a lot of good research now. (However, you should avoid using the term "parental alienation syndrome," which is not widely accepted.) Reading this book will help you deal with alienating behaviors by your ex and is based on a lot of research.

Second, as a therapist and then as a lawyer, I learned about "personality disorders" in 1980, and this has been the focus of a lot of my work since then. I believe that most parents who engage in extreme alienating behaviors have personality disorders, which are generally repeated patterns of dysfunctional interpersonal behavior in close relationships that include emotional instability, impulsiveness, and distorted perceptions of themselves, others, and events. About ten percent of adults have personality disorders, and their patterns of behavior fit much of what Lisa and Chris talk about in this book. But you should generally avoid talking about "personality disorders" in court or with your ex. Instead, with professionals, focus on "concerning patterns of behavior" and describe specific behaviors that are undermining your relationship with your child or children. This book teaches a lot about those specific behaviors.

An important aspect of personality disorders is that people with them generally act impulsively out of their disorders rather than logically thinking through their actions. They also do not reflect on their own behavior and think about changing it. Instead, if they get negative feedback, they become highly defensive and more aggressive, not less. So when Lisa and Chris talk about such parents' "intentional" behavior, it is not the same as your intentional behavior. It is not something that you (or even a judge) can successfully argue with or talk them out of. Instead, what is needed is setting limits and imposing consequences as soon as possible after alienating behaviors begin.

With those two points made, I want to encourage you to absorb the information you are about to read and follow the suggestions that Lisa and Chris make in this book. They have done an excellent job of providing knowledge combined with supportive comments that should help any parent in this difficult situation. The patterns of this problem are very predictable, and the solutions are as well. There is hope!

**Bill Eddy, LCSW, Esq.**
Director of Innovation at the High Conflict Institute
Author, *Don't Alienate the Kids* and *Splitting: Protecting Yourself While Divorcing Someone with Borderline or Narcissistic Personality Disorders*

# INTRODUCTION

> *"No matter what you think of the other party, these children are one-half of each of you. Remember that, because every time you tell your child what an 'idiot' his father is, or what a 'fool' his mother is, you are telling the child half of him is bad."*
>
> —Minnesota Judge Michael Haas, in a 2001 ruling

When we began our work as high-conflict divorce, custody, and co-parenting strategists, we were focused on *legal abuse* – the consistent pattern of weaponization of the family court system by abusive personality types during and after the divorce and separation process. Legal abuse is the subject of our first book, *Been There Got Out: Toxic Relationships, High-Conflict Divorce, and How to Stay Sane Under Insane Circumstances*.

We quickly noticed another consistent, horrific pattern: the weaponization of *children*.

A former partner intentionally influencing your child to reject, fear, or severely distance themselves from you is *"parental alienation."* We'll get deeper into exactly what this means in the opening chapter.

There is nothing we see in our work that causes more pain for parents, and the damage done to children can have a lifelong impact. Toxic people are a nightmare to deal with in the family court system. They'll make false accusations, hide money, refuse to cooperate with the process, and do anything to maintain the power and control that existed in the relationship. The worst is when they undermine your relationship with your children. They see kids just like they see money: both are part of the spoils of war and it's a war that you must lose.

In our coaching practice, we deal exclusively with the abnormal. The people in our community suffer emotional abuse at a minimum, and in nearly every case, the root cause is some sort of mental health issue their partner has, most commonly *narcissism*, which, in technical psychology terms, is a "Cluster B" personality disorder.

We are not mental health professionals, so we don't diagnose anyone, but the behaviors are remarkably consistent. Throughout this book, when we use words like *narcissist* or *toxic*, we're describing patterns of behavior, not offering a diagnosis that you don't need, won't get, and wouldn't help anyway.

It's normal for separating partners to be angry and resentful toward each other, and few people can navigate the process without the kids sensing at least a bit of conflict. But most parents come to see how important it is not to put them in the middle. Most loving parents with at least a bit of emotional maturity settle down, start to think about the next chapter of their lives, and focus on figuring out how to co-parent as effectively as possible. Children take some lumps, but they can usually be OK in time.

Not so with the exes in our orbit. When your relationship with a toxic partner ends, they rarely just move on.

## The Controversy Around Alienation:

> "*I think the misconception of alienation comes from the fear that when men face allegations of abuse, they deflect by claiming, 'No, the children are only saying that I was abusive because their mom alienated them.'*"
>
> — **Ashish Joshi, Attorney**

If you have already begun to research alienation before picking up this book, you have probably seen how polarizing the topic is. There are several "experts" with large online followings who insist that parental alienation doesn't even exist, despite all the evidence to the contrary.

We find this incredibly foolish, small-minded, and, worst of all, harmful to the parents who are living with alienation and desperately looking for help. Why would anyone deny that such a demonstrably real problem exists? The core issue is a misapplication of the concept in a family court system that lacks the sophistication to distinguish between valid cases of parental alienation and false accusations of it.

Toxic partners aren't just abusive towards you; they're *inherently* abusive and can be abusive towards anyone, including their kids. So, when you're in a custody battle and filled with fear about how you'll be able to protect your children post-separation, you may focus your legal narrative on how horrible your soon-to-be ex is and how the court needs to keep your kids safe.

This runs counter to the core value of the family court of wanting both parents to retain important roles in kids' lives. And opposing counsel will pounce, leading to something we call the *Protective Parent Spin Cycle*, which we get into in Chapter 1.

When you claim that your ex is abusing your kids, but can't definitively prove it, you open the door for the other side to falsely accuse you of alienation, often to devastating effect.

Chris had a brief glimpse of how deeply this dynamic has become entrenched in the legal system when he switched attorneys mid-divorce. In their first strategy session, his new lawyer asked whether Chris' ex was accusing him of abuse. (She wasn't.) The attorney said, "Well, if she does, we'll just counter with parental alienation."

This was years ago, and we hadn't yet educated ourselves on this subject. Still, on some level, Chris felt terribly uneasy with this reflexive reaction from one of the most respected lawyers in his jurisdiction, who wasn't even familiar with the details of the case yet.

Parental alienation can be a powerful weapon in the court system, and lawyers know it. To some, the objective validity of their argument is secondary to getting a win.

All of this leads to a legal environment where the entirely valid concept of parental alienation is regularly weaponized by abusers in the form of false claims that a protective parent is alienating the children, when all they're really trying to do is keep their kids safe; they're just going about it the wrong way.

Many movements are born from injustice. The anti-alienation people are justifiably angry at how alienation is weaponized, but their anger has taken them so far that they reject the entire concept, to the detriment of a huge group of parents who are dealing with real cases of alienation every single day.

## What Lawyers Say

We interview attorneys all the time for our podcast and social media channels, and they are the ones working in the trenches of family court. Ashish Joshi, a domestic violence attorney specializing in alienation, told us that it is very common for someone being accused of alienation to bring in an expert who tries to challenge the whole theory, saying that it doesn't have scientific support or enough empirical research. That in itself is false because there is an overwhelming amount of peer-reviewed research out there.

In one of his cases, the judge became frustrated with the back and forth about whether alienation exists. She asked the expert witness if alienation *never* happens—if there's *no such thing*. The expert started to backtrack, saying it does happen *in some situations*. When questioned further, the expert admitted that sometimes parents do engage in behaviors that can cause harm to a child. The judge asked what those behaviors were and if they had been observed in a clinical setting. The expert admitted they had been, going on to describe the very same behaviors noted by psychologist, author, and pioneering parental alienation expert, Dr. Amy Baker, which we discuss throughout this book.

## Our Advice to You

We didn't come into this with any agenda. We care only about helping people deal with getting out of toxic relationships, especially in the legal system, and in navigating the treacherous waters of co-parenting with high-conflict exes. In our work, we've learned two critical lessons when it comes to parental alienation: First, no matter how alienation has been misapplied at times in someone else's case, the undermining behavior we explore in this book is real, and it's actually common in our community. We have seen it time and time again. Abuse isn't a gender issue, a socioeconomic issue, or a geographical issue. People in any demographic group can have toxic personality disorders. This is a global problem that can affect anyone. Second, the concept of parental alienation can be a formidable weapon in family court, whether we like it or not. So, you better know what it is, you better be ready to defend yourself against false accusations of it, and you damn sure better not do it yourself, even accidentally.

In short, burying your head in the sand and dismissing parental alienation as some sort of fiction is asking for trouble and putting your children and yourself in serious jeopardy of a long list of very bad things. Your children and your relationship with them are at stake. You need to be laser-focused and grounded in reality.

## Educating Yourself is the First Step

The absolute best thing you can do is to educate yourself. Surprisingly few therapists understand alienation, even when obvious symptoms are present. The same applies to parenting coordinators, custody evaluators, guardians ad litem, judges, and others who may have a significant role in your custody and co-parenting situation. So few lawyers understand the particulars of parental alienation to the degree needed to litigate it effectively when it's happening, at least without help, that we refer to those who can as *unicorns*. If you're going to be successful, you have two choices: find a unicorn, or *be* the unicorn.

We work with our clients to help them take strategic oversight of their cases. That doesn't mean you go rogue on your attorney, but it does mean that you're the one who must step up and fill in the gaps in their knowledge and expertise. The simple fact is that the court isn't built to handle the nuances of cases involving alienation, and nobody's going to change the system fast enough to make a difference in yours.

## Practical, Actionable Advice

The fact that you're holding this book is a great first step. Most of the credible information available on alienation consists of scholarly papers in the mental health sciences or technical legal publications…not the most accessible sources. If you're about to be eaten by a bear, it's not particularly helpful to learn about their habitat or mating habits. You need to know, *right now*, how to defend yourself against its attack.

In writing this book, as in all of our work, our goal is to give you actionable advice that you can use to help yourself if you're dealing with alienation. It's your *Bear Attack Survival Guide*, and it's especially necessary because a lot of the park rangers around here will tell you that bears don't exist.

We've curated our advice from extensive research, interviews with hundreds of experts—from family law attorneys to psychologists to custody evaluators—our personal experiences, and our case work with our clients. We give you an extensive set of tools and tips that you can put into action to make your situation better in real life if you're unfortunate enough to be facing this terrible problem.

Let's start right away with this tip: **Don't ever give up.** Giving up on your relationship with your child becomes a self-fulfilling prophecy, and is the one thing that has the greatest potential to hand a twisted victory to your ex.

Even the worst cases of alienation can be undone in time. It won't be easy. It will almost certainly be a marathon. So you need a marathon mindset. And a plan.

Let's get to it!

# CHAPTER 1

# ALIENATION VS. ESTRANGEMENT

*"Our attachment systems are very rich. They don't really fracture unless there's a huge force put upon them."*

—Adam Barta, Social Worker

**Kim's Story**

Kim's parents separated when she was still in diapers, and her mother consistently portrayed her father as a "con artist and liar" who only showed interest when he needed something. Her dad struggled to support himself financially throughout his life and had been jailed intermittently for failing to pay child support.

Her mother remarried a man who blamed Kim for her mother's unhappiness and stress. There was a lot of back-and-forth in the legal system between her parents, and every time court stuff came up, her stepfather would lash out at Kim. Whenever she'd visit her dad, she'd come home to some kind of retribution, often her stepdad berating her, "**You're just like your father.**"

When she was twelve, Kim discovered a stack of documents related to her parents' extensive legal wrangling. She had no clue what they meant, but it had become clear that any remaining connection she had with her father was causing distress in her mother's home. Not long afterward, Kim was called into the judge's chambers during yet another court appearance. When asked about her preference regarding visitation with her dad, she replied that she would "do anything to make my mother stop crying."

Her father got the message; shortly after, he signed away his parental rights, which relieved him of child support obligations but barred him from seeing Kim legally until she turned eighteen.

Despite the agreement, she would occasionally catch glimpses of him showing up at the school bus stop, which confused her. Afraid of what might happen, Kim would stay on the bus for an extra stop when she saw her father there. Kim's grandmother on her dad's side tried to initiate a reconciliation and would sometimes invite Kim over to her house. But when her father showed up, Kim was torn—she knew her mother would be furious if she developed any relationship with her dad.

He'd tried contacting her when she was in college. As an adult, on her birthday, she would sometimes find flowers on her car windshield that she knew were from him.

Starting in high school, every guy Kim dated was older. She now understands that she was looking for her father in a partner. She ended up marrying a man whose most compelling attribute was making her feel safe. When Kim was in her early thirties, her husband got a call that her father was dying. If she wanted to see him, it would have to happen immediately. As her husband drove her into the hospital parking lot, the thought in Kim's mind was her mother's words: "Dad only wants you when he needs something." She could not bring herself to go inside and face him, and shortly thereafter, her father died. She has regretted this decision ever since.

Kim is still struck by how pivotal moments like these affect everything—her comment to a judge as a twelve-year-old essentially ended her relationship with her father. Permanently. She reflects now on how she felt like a bumper car being bounced and banged back and forth, which impacted the future trajectory of her life in profound ways, including who she chose to spend it with. She is very conflict-avoidant to this day. Kim's mother passed away while we were writing this book, and her grief is mixed with resentment.

One good thing that came out of all of this was Kim's discovery a few years ago when she took a genetic test, which revealed she had three older brothers, including a set of identical twins—her father's children from a prior relationship. She now has relationships with her half-brothers, one of whom she speaks with all the time, and another, whom she adores, is a mentor for her son as he starts his professional career.

## The Strong Parent/Child Bonds

As human beings, we are biologically wired to want to connect to other people. This bond is unique when it comes to our parents—the first connections we make in life are with them. On the day we're born, there's not much we can do without help, whether it's eating, changing our diapers, or controlling whether we are warm or cold. This dependency exists before birth; we attach to others who can help us meet these basic needs. A child's foundational bond with a parent is extremely hard to break.

## Estrangement

What could so severely damage this bond that a child would choose to reject their mother or father, an inherently unnatural act? Sometimes, a parent's behavior is the cause, by being unsupportive, uninvolved, abusive, or neglectful. Any of these could lead to a child choosing to cut off contact. This is what's known as *justified estrangement*. In situations like these, the mother's or father's conduct created a rift so profound that it ultimately outweighed the fundamental need for connection that every child has with their parents. *That's not what this book is about.*

## Alienation

Sometimes, the damage is done intentionally by someone else, and this is one of the most common things we see in our work with clients.

When you separate from an emotionally disordered partner, they cannot process the end of the relationship as a healthy person would. They may then make it their mission to destroy you by whatever means possible. And children, unfortunately, lack the maturity to protect themselves against insidious manipulation from someone they're hard-wired to trust.

The combination creates the perfect environment for your ex to intentionally undermine your relationship with your kids. *That's alienation, and that is what this book is about.*

An alienating parent engages in patterns of behavior by doing things like badmouthing the "targeted" parent (you) or interfering with your access time. Even if your ex's behavior isn't enough to fully sever the relationship, it can still cause a wide range of problems that affect the entire family. When the alienation is severe, your kid may completely detach from and reject everything associated with you.

The list of alienating behaviors is long, and we'll get into a lot more detail throughout this book.

## How Can You Tell?

Even professionals struggle to figure it out. Psychologist Dr. Amy Baker says the key is examining the *cause* of the child's disaffection. Is it organic due to something within the relationship? Then it's probably *estrangement*. But if it's imposed on the child by the other parent, there's a good chance it's *alienation*.

Clinical professor of psychiatry Dr. Richard Warshak notes that pathological alienation—the most extreme—occurs when a child develops what he calls an "unreasonable aversion" to a parent with whom the child formerly had an affectionate, normal relationship with after the other parent shares their negative attitudes about that person. In his book, *Litigating Parental Alienation*, attorney Ashish Joshi uses the following criteria to distinguish behaviors of moderately to severely alienated children from those that do not indicate alienation:

1. **The negative messages from your ex to your children are frequent, consistent, and chronic, versus occasional.** Divorce is a time of intense emotions. It's normal for a parent to take a while to learn how to shield a child from the anger or resentment you're feeling towards your ex. Ongoing negativity over time is a different story. This is about patterns, not isolated incidents.
2. **Your child's negativity is directed only at you, not at both you and your ex.** They have a distorted idea that you are evil, dangerous, or undeserving of their love or attention, while their relationship with your ex is largely unaffected.
3. **What your child says or does is not reflective of their typical developmental stage.** When they use language or express a view that doesn't sound like their own, it's quite likely that your ex planted it in their head.
4. **Your child's response is not justified by anything you've done, past or present.** If your relationship was good before things got bad with your ex, and you didn't do

anything terrible, the natural bond you have with your child should rule the day…unless there's something else going on.

Alienation coach Charlie McCready breaks it down more simply: ***Estrangement*** is when you do something that damages your relationship with your child. ***Alienation*** is when your co-parent is intentionally damaging your relationship with your child by forcing them into a loyalty conflict where they have to choose one of you over the other.

Adam Barta, founder of Head in the Right Direction Counseling Services, told us about a child he was seeing who, now in fifth grade, said he hated his father and wanted nothing to do with him because he "didn't buy me the crayons I wanted when I was in third grade." That flimsy explanation is a red flag that more is going on beneath the surface than art supplies.

Florida attorney Charles Jamieson has been litigating alienation cases for decades, and thinks of them in what he calls *bookends*. At one end is the solid relationship you always had with your child. At the other end are allegations that they now want nothing to do with you. The question in the middle is, what's the reason?

According to Canadian psychologist and researcher Nicholas Bala, in high-conflict separations, sometimes both parents attempt to undermine their child's relationship with the other parent. However, it's only a minority of cases where children vehemently reject one parent and resist or even refuse contact.

## The Alienation Factors

We mentioned in the introduction how the misapplication of the concept of parental alienation in the legal system has spawned a small army of internet trolls who would have us all believe that parental alienation doesn't even exist. Most judges, lawyers, and court professionals don't generally share that view. When it comes to the legal system, Ashish Joshi says that the courts aren't interested in a theoretical debate about what's real or not. They want effective solutions to address bad co-parenting behavior.

Dr. Amy Baker is an internationally recognized expert on parent-child attachment issues, and in her book, *Co-Parenting with a Toxic Ex*, she and co-author Paul Fine present a list of seventeen factors that indicate the presence of parental alienation. In our work with clients, we condense these down to six categories (we'll get into more depth on these in Chapters 4 and 5). The categories are:

1. **Sending poisonous messages about you.** This is a big one. It covers all the signals your ex is sending to your children, whether they snicker derisively at your comment in a child's therapy session, assure the kids that they can always call if they "don't feel safe" with you, or plant seeds of doubt by saying something like, "I hope Dad comes to your game; I know he's busy with his new girlfriend."

   Essentially, your ex wants to give your kid the impression that you are what we call the "three U's:"
   - Unsafe
   - Unloving
   - Unavailable

   The underlying idea is that you are not only a bad parent but a bad person.

2. **Interfering with contact and communication.** This is anything they do that impedes your ability to have an

independent, healthy parenting relationship with your kids, including:

- Obstructing your court-ordered access time by not following the schedule, claiming the kids are busy or don't want to see you, or regularly disrupting your time together by contacting them when you're in the middle of something fun.
- Blocking your number on the kids' phones, missing scheduled phone calls or Facetimes, or lurking when you're talking with them so the children can't speak freely, and come to associate your conversations with discomfort.
- Positioning themselves as a liaison between you and your kid, which prevents you from having open conversations or working out conflicts directly.

3. **Erasing and replacing.** Toxic exes often attempt to rewrite history to make your child feel like you were never as loving or involved as you really were. They'll try to minimize your role in your child's life. This includes trying to change a child's name during a divorce, or encouraging them to call their new partner some version of Mom or Dad.

Your ex may reinvent your family's history, minimizing your role or failing to mention your involvement. Although it's normal to clean the house of your ex's pictures after a divorce, your ex may wipe all traces of you, even from your kids' room. The real motivation behind this is to erase you from their minds.

4. **Encouraging a child to betray your trust.** Your ex may interrogate your child about what goes on during their

time with you or encourage them to spy and report back, which puts intense strain on your relationship by putting them in the middle. When kids betray you as little spies, your ex rewards them emotionally. One of our client's teenage daughters would eavesdrop on her mom's phone conversations and relay details to her father. When our client asked why, her candid answer was, "It's the only way I can get Dad to pay attention to me."

5. **Undermining your authority.** Ever notice how your ex acts like they are in charge? Alienating parents will make children feel that they're the only parent whose rules matter, no matter whose parenting time it is. A child experiencing this may say things like, "I need to check with Mom," or "Dad says I can't have donuts on Sunday mornings anymore."

6. **Fostering dependence in your child.** One of our most important roles as parents is to teach our kids how to live in the world without us, to help them become self-sufficient. A toxic parent often wants the opposite.

Parental alienation is not a misunderstanding or a mistake. It is a deliberate, calculated strategy driven by deep-seated psychological needs for control, power, revenge, and a profound lack of empathy for your children.

## Stages of Alienation

The impact of alienation occurs on a spectrum. Broadly speaking, you can think of three stages when it comes to severity:

**Mild.** When your child continues to see you but is starting to complain, portrays events inaccurately, or shows new resistance to you, these are signs that some fractures are beginning to develop in your relationship, according to Ashish Joshi. At this stage, your child may come to you all bent out of shape, but once parenting time is underway, they'll mostly bounce back and enjoy their time with you.

**Moderate.** Here, your child starts to strongly resist contact and is "persistently oppositional" during parenting time, says Joshi. Kids may become very disrespectful, disobey your rules, and make statements about not feeling safe or comfortable with you. They might disengage, hide in their room, and stop sharing anything about their life. It might take longer for them to warm up, if they warm up at all.

**Severe.** According to Charlie McCready, this level of withdrawal occurs when your child just can't stand up to all the pressure from your alienating ex. As hard as it is to break their bond with you, it has become harder to risk displeasing their other parent, and the kids may begin to make cruel statements like:

- "You do not exist."
- "I wish you were not my father or my mother."
- "I wish you were dead."

They demonstrate that they are internalizing the nasty things that your ex is drilling into them. We have now unfortunately crossed into the worst level of alienation, where a child regularly wants no contact, becomes hysterical if you show up at school, or even calls 911. These situations require very different interventions from mild or moderate cases.

Regardless of how far things have progressed, hope is not lost, but you will have an easier time fighting back the earlier you see what's going on and take decisive action to stop it. As we often say, it's easier to prevent a spill than to clean one up. If you can get out in front of this and nip it in the bud, you and your children will be better off.

## The Protective Parent Spin Cycle

If mental health professionals struggle to figure out what's really happening when they're hearing opposite stories from parents who both come across as sincere and truthful, what chance does a judge have, considering that they have no time to delve deep and lack the necessary skills and experience? On top of all of that, we see as many incidents of a healthy parent being falsely accused of alienation as we do bona fide alienation cases, and we commonly see plenty of cases with both dynamics happening at the same time: our client's ex is alienating the kids while simultaneously making false accusations of the same thing in court. All of this leads to a terrible sequence that we've seen play out time and time again, which we call *The Protective Parent Spin Cycle*. It goes like this:

1. A toxic parent neglects or abuses a child.
2. The protective parent responds strongly (who among us wouldn't?) and does whatever they believe they have to do to make it stop, including reporting to CPS (Child Protective Services) or the police, filing emergency motions, or, maybe in violation of custody orders, refusing to send the child to the abuser.
3. Investigations by authorities fail to produce proof of the abuse—remember what we just said about how hard it is for professionals to figure out who's telling the truth?
4. When things aren't crystal clear, the case gets closed with a status of unfounded, which does not necessarily

mean *pro*ven false, but rather, we don't have enough to say for sure.

5. Regardless, the abusive parent and their aggressive attorney strut into court and say, "SEE? You made all of these allegations up! I was proven to have done nothing wrong! You're just bitter and vindictive, and you're the reason the kids don't want to see me—that's parental alienation, and I deserve full custody!"

It's astonishing how often this happens. We have a client whose preschooler claimed that their father had been inappropriately touching them, and by the time we met, *The Protective Parent Spin Cycle* had already played out. Our client had filed multiple motions and been aggressive in court, which backfired, leading to a change from her having full physical and legal custody to only a few hours a week of supervised visitation. A judge had ruled that since there had been multiple unfounded claims, her behavior was not only unwarranted but damaging to her child, as well as to the child's relationship with her ex.

In trying to move forward, she had no choice but to recant all of the accusations she had made and agree to take no further action of the kind. She has since taken multiple parenting classes, gotten three psychological evaluations, and been a model citizen on every single supervised visit, all showing that she is fine. Nonetheless, she still must claw her way slowly out of this deep, dark hole just to get back to 50/50.

### It's Not Good Enough, But it's What We Have

This kind of thing happens regularly in our crazy world (and we know you know). It starts with what we talked about already: the justice system (broadly speaking) lacks the sophistication to sort out whose story is true. And, since your ex is probably very comfortable on the stage that the family court offers, while you may be so emotionally distraught that you struggle to keep your composure, the other side can come across as more credible.

A lot of times, opposing counsel will tell a story of how you, in your vindictive rage, are trying to destroy your ex's relationship with your kids. And when the kids confirmed your story of abuse to a custody evaluator? They were coached by you! Their reports of your ex's behavior are used as further proof of how awful you are. It's the opposite of the truth, but, unfortunately, it can play well in this environment. This is what has the anti-alienation faction all bent out of shape and denying that alienation even exists.

We'll often say to people that we don't waste time lamenting the broken family court system. We're all for change and reform, and when a good solution comes along, we'll get behind it. But that's going to take a long time, and right now, you have a serious problem to deal with, and you need to do all you can to be successful in this bizarre environment.

So, one of our first pieces of advice is to avoid doomscrolling. Don't pour the energy you will need for more productive activities into all the negativity online. The truth is that shocking stories are the exception, and your own personal horror story is probably avoidable if you can learn how to conduct yourself properly, both in and out of the court system.

### Three Problems to Solve

All of this leaves you with potentially three main problems that require a solution. You'll need to:

1. **Get the best co-parenting arrangement** you possibly can in light of your ex's alienating behaviors while avoiding the *Protective Parent Spin Cycle*, whether or not alienation is part of your narrative in court.

2. **Insulate yourself against their false claims** that you're alienating the kids from them.
3. **Protect your relationships with your children** against your ex's insidious campaign to destroy them.

Many people we meet who are facing a situation like this use the word "overwhelmed" to describe how they feel, and trust us, we get it. Take a breath. It's bad, but there's a lot you can do, and that's why we wrote this book.

### Questions for Reflection

1. Looking at the criteria for distinguishing alienation from estrangement, what evidence do you have that your child's rejection is being imposed by your ex rather than stemming organically from your relationship? (Consider the frequency of negative messages, whether they are directed only at you, and whether your child's responses match their developmental stage.)
2. Before your separation, what was the quality of your relationship with your child? (Think about moments which highlight your relationship, involvement, and positive interactions that demonstrate this rejection represents a significant change from the way things were before things soured with your ex.)
3. Which of the six alienation factors (poisonous messages, interfering with contact, erasing/replacing, encouraging betrayal, undermining authority, fostering dependence) do you recognize in your situation? Choose the most prominent one and identify three specific examples that demonstrate this pattern of behavior.

## CHAPTER 2

# THE IMPACT OF ALIENATION

*"Kids who reject a loving, protective parent often feel rejected themselves on some level, because they have been tricked into believing that you are the one rejecting them."*

—Dr. Amy Baker, Psychologist

### Children Learn to Read the Room

Children who are abused learn to repress their feelings. They are not allowed to express anger or sadness because they might get in trouble. Instead, they learn to read the room. In social settings, they pay close attention to everybody else's emotions, keeping their own in check to stay safe, says Canadian therapist and author Marnie Grundman.

They learn to watch other adults, particularly an abusive parent, and understand there's a "silent language" being expressed at all times. They become acutely aware of how their own face looks and whether they are allowed to speak or make eye contact while continuously monitoring their environment. This, of course, leaves no room to process feelings that they are not even allowed to have.

Clinical psychologist and former president of the Cincinnati Academy of Psychology, Dr. David Marcus, notes that children are exquisitely aware of how their parents feel. They may find themselves acting as pleasers, placaters, and sometimes even messengers, which can be harmfully inappropriate roles for kids. Even very young children feel the hostility, and what's worse is that they don't understand why and can end up blaming themselves for it. What bothers them most? The yelling. This is why they often retreat to their bedrooms and hide beneath the covers or in a closet. Anything to get away from the conflict.

## The Filter

When a child is being emotionally manipulated by a parent, understand that all of their decisions, opinions, goals, and preferences are filtered through the needs of that person.

Grundman notes that children who grow up in environments like this may just "check out" or dissociate in a larger social setting because it's too much stimulation and they are afraid that someone is going to reject, dislike, or judge them.

Kids in narcissistic family systems often also develop a sense of self-reliance, which can lead them to insulate themselves. They may become adults who are unable to ask for help, or cannot accept kindness or praise because it's so foreign.

The kicker, Grundman says, is that when anything good happens, the trauma that lives in their bodies sends a signal that something bad is going to follow, because their entire life experience throughout childhood has been this way. The fracturing of a natural parental bond will have a significant impact on your child's current relationships, as well as their future attachments, including friendships and romantic partners. The good news is that kids are by no means condemned to becoming narcissists themselves, nor doomed to a future full of toxic relationships.

They *can* turn out just fine. But it's going to take a special effort by you to give them the best chance of becoming emotionally healthy adults. The fact that you're aware of what the problem is and you're educating yourself is a very hopeful sign, because inaction could be tragic.

### The Impact Runs Broad & Deep

High-conflict divorce can cause a *spontaneous disruption* to the attachment system.

Imagine that two gods are fighting over you. It's that big for children, says social worker Adam Barta. The two people that they are most attached to are in such conflict that they no longer feel safe. As a way to resolve it, they must choose one regardless of their attachment to the other.

From the perspective of someone who understands trauma, these behaviors are probably normal given what's going on in the family dynamics. Psychologist and author Dr. Josh Coleman notes that a variety of influences play a role in determining with whom a child aligns. Kids may choose your ex due to the *weight of their own empathy*, feeling sorry for their other parent, because they sense that your ex's happiness depends on them, while yours doesn't.

A lot also depends on your child's developmental stage. Older kids may be trying to pull away from your "orbit," and simply crave independence, or might perceive your ex as less demanding and prefer an environment with fewer rules. We see many teenagers choose to go with the parent who allows them more autonomy. Plus, it's human nature to want what we can't have. Many children will reject healthy, loving parents because they idealize a father or mother who is not as emotionally available. Chris' parents split up when he was twelve, and his dad essentially abandoned him for a life with the new family he started. Well into adulthood, Chris spent a lot of energy chasing his father down an emotional one-way street. He learned that love was something to be pursued, which contributed to him becoming a vulnerable target for his ex later on. Your kids already feel responsible for the split. Their desire to avoid conflict can contribute to withdrawal. Understanding the child's perspective will help you realize how much struggle is beneath the surface.

## Cognitive Dissonance

Kids, especially younger ones, have a narrow world; their views and opinions are initially shaped by their parents, and only later do they draw from a wider pool of influencers. This is why our children tend to at least start life sharing our values, rooting for the same sports teams, and using our language and expressions. Nature has programmed them to model themselves after us because it's their best chance for survival in the world.

When parents express negative perceptions of each other, a child gets two different, conflicting stories to sort out, leaving no mental space for them to develop their own perception. Broadly speaking, cognitive dissonance is the discomfort that we feel when experiencing conflicting beliefs at the same time. In the context of this book, it's your child's contradictory emotions. On one hand, there's the strong natural bond they have with you, combined with the observable evidence of your love; on the other, it's the aforementioned "huge force" that their other parent, whom they also have a strong natural bond with, is exerting on them.

But now one parent who is a master manipulator, maybe subtly at first, is signaling that the other parent is bad, in direct conflict with your child's internal wiring and quite likely their early life experience. Kids don't know how to resolve this irresistible force meeting this immovable object, leading to intense internal conflict.

## The Damage

Research from a wide range of sources has consistently found a variety of developmental and psychological problems in children who are being alienated from a parent. Kids in these situations often experience:

- Anxiety and depression
- Low self-esteem
- Guilt and shame (for rejecting the targeted parent)
- Impaired ability to trust themselves or others, stemming from the disorienting effects of gaslighting and a distorted perception of reality
- Trauma/PTSD
- Isolation

Your love is unconditional. They can be little monsters with you. But in their efforts to navigate a relationship with an unhealthy parent, kids do what they need to do to survive. With your ex, they need to develop their version of "walking on eggshells" to keep the peace. They may create a whole persona for that purpose, and the risk becomes that this superficial approach, borne out of necessity, can spill over to their other relationships.

With all the emotional turmoil in the family, kids often get derailed academically. As an aside, the silver lining to that particular cloud is that sometimes school will notice and steer a child towards some kind of counseling, which can potentially be an opportunity to get your child the help you haven't been able to get them otherwise.

**The Elephant in the Room**

One of the biggest fears expressed in our community is, "How can my child possibly be OK with a parent like that?" Underneath this is the angst that a child who spends significant time in the custody of a narcissistic parent without you acting as a buffer will be destroyed. This fear can be further exacerbated by the fact that kids can sometimes act like little narcissists as part of their normal development.

When a problematic parent's emotional manipulation is not addressed, the dynamics that can bloom into alienation include:

1. **Internalizing the narcissistic parent's dynamics.** In other words, the apple doesn't fall far from the tree; a child picks up behaviors modeled for them.
2. **Going through cycles of idealization and devaluation**, along with all the other dysfunctional machinations of relationships with narcissists, just as you may have experienced. The inconsistency and conditional nature of that parent's love for your child can lead to insecurity and a desperate need for validation from alternative, external sources, a common feature of narcissism.
3. **The narcissistic parent's lack of empathy directly affects their parenting** through an inability to authentically recognize their child's emotions. Our parents are our first models for basically everything, including our relationships with others, and one of your child's two primary models for relationships is severely empathy-deficient.

4. **A parent's sense of entitlement.** People like your ex consider themselves special and believe they should be treated as such. And so should their kids, who can develop their own sense of privilege.
5. **A parent's focus on power and control, especially through manipulation.** A child growing up with this dynamic may learn that this is how they'll be able to get what they want throughout life.

Of course, it's way more complex than that, and this is not a psychology textbook. What's most important to understand is that, in a shared custody situation where a child is spending time with both of you, we're pretty certain that your co-parent is not going to do their part in raising an emotionally healthy child. That's the bad news. The good news is that you probably have a chance at countering these effects through your exceptional parenting, including the empathy, accountability, and emotional regulation (and more, of course) that made you a target for your ex in the first place.

While we're at it, let's do some myth-busting. Some people express to us that they wish they had stayed in the relationship because, at least then, they'd be able to "protect" the kids from the other parent. Logical as that may seem, what you're really modeling for your kids when you stay is, *This is OK. This is normal. This is what relationships look like.* Probably not what you had in mind.

When you get out, move on, and begin to heal, however it happens, you're showing your kids who you really are, without all the hoops you had to jump through just to keep the peace when you were still with your ex.

If you're fortunate enough to find healthy love at some point, as the two of us did when we met each other, you might even have the opportunity to model a very different relationship dynamic for your kids. In our case, the four total children the two of us have from our marriages have seen us together for more than half their lives.

So, try not to worry too much about whether your child will become a narcissist. If you can overcome the alienation campaign and preserve your role in your child's life, that's most important, and it will open the door for you to solve other problems that might come up over the years.

## The Child's Perspective: Two Sisters

We had a unique opportunity to interview two sisters, both young adults, who were separated from their mother for eight years by an intensive alienation campaign by their father, who had been working to undermine the girls' relationships with her well before the separation. Mom had full custody until an incident where she lost her temper with her elder daughter, Paige, and Dad seized the opportunity to blow the incident out of proportion in the legal system.

These were originally two separate interviews, but we've made edits for readability purposes and changed their names. You can listen to or watch the full interviews on our Been There Got Out podcast or YouTube channel.

**Paige:** My parents got divorced when I was about seven years old, and then my father took me away from my mom when I was fourteen, turning fifteen years old.

**Amanda:** Me and my sister were living with my mom after our parents' divorce, and we had visitations with my dad. Something that appealed to my sister and me as children was that he didn't have any rules. As a child, you don't really know the consequences of spoiling. As children, Dad was always our favorite because he was the cool parent—we got to watch TV, eat junk food, and do no homework. So we always enjoyed spending time with him. And every time we went to visit, he would basically always just talk really negatively about my mom. He painted this image into our heads that she's crazy, she's so strict, she doesn't let you have fun. The more time we spent with him, the more he would just talk about how much he disliked our mom and how she's crazy, she makes you do your homework, she makes you brush your teeth. As kids, we were like, yeah, that's annoying. As my sister became fifteen, my dad basically convinced her that she didn't have to really take care of herself.

**Paige:** It actually happened a long time before that. For as long as I can remember, my father had always been saying very negative things to me about my mother, always making her out to be the enemy, even before I left living with my mom. He always put in my head, If you lived with me, our life would be so different.

**Amanda:** He would always talk about my mom and how she's a horrible parent and "Oh, she cheated on me, she doesn't love you guys, she doesn't love me, and the reason why this family is gonna fall apart is because of your mom, because she's sleeping with other men." He never had really a good thing to say about anyone, just, "Oh, everyone did this to me," so he was a perpetual victim. He would always just talk about [my mom] for years on end, about how she did this, she doesn't love me, she cheated, and stuff like that.

**Lisa:** You said they divorced when you were four and you're twenty. So, sixteen years later, he's still cycling about her.

**Amanda:** Yeah, like fixated on her, and the thing is, it's not just her, it's just his personality type, like a lot of unresolved trauma; he would still obsess about things that happened when he was a teenager. All I heard was, "She's a bad person, she doesn't love this family." Since I was a baby, those thoughts were already implanted in my head, so I automatically always saw her through negative eyes.

**Paige:** When I was fourteen, I was pretty rebellious. It was the beginning of puberty, and I had a conflict with my mother. There was a guy that I was talking to, and that made me really focused on him, and I didn't really care about how my mother would feel if I talked to her a certain way. That's when things got very tense between us. We had a disagreement, and my mom kind of smacked me. I don't really hold it against her now. But that's when my father took the opportunity to say, "Your mother's abusive, your mother beat you half to death," when she didn't. He reported her for child abuse and neglect. And that's when he took the opportunity to take us away from her.

It was so unexpected when it happened. It was over something stupid, like I was yelling at her, and she didn't really know what else to do, so she kind of reacted. And that's when I told my dad, "Mom hit me." So he called the police, had her taken away in handcuffs, and was like, "Okay, we're gonna get a restraining order."

**Amanda:** So then my sister called him, and my dad was like, "Don't do anything, just wait until I get there." He used that as, "Okay, I'm gonna call the police on you, they're gonna arrest you because you put your hands on my daughter."

They arrested her, and then we went to live with my dad. They said that it was gonna just be two days, but since she was in jail, he used it as an opportunity to get a restraining order and was telling us, "Oh, you see, she doesn't love you guys, she hit you, she doesn't care about you, she doesn't want to take care of you."

When my sister and my mom were arguing, my mom used to say, "If you want to live with your dad, then go live with your dad." I thought that was a genuine opportunity. I didn't really think there was anything wrong with it, because she had often told us, "Since you love him so much, then go live with him."

**Paige:** Everything happened so fast. It was all within like a day. I woke up, this happened, and then, before I knew it, I never went back to that house. I felt as if this was all my fault, and because of that, I didn't really want to see my mom, because I thought that if I were to see her again, she would hate me for it. It was very unexpected. I was almost in shock that day, watching everything happen so quickly. My sister was also a part of it. She didn't really have a say in anything. I think it was more unfair to her because she just went along with what happened. She didn't really get to choose; she just followed me. That also made me feel guilty to think that, because of me, my sister was also part of not being able to talk to my mom.

Ever since that day, my father has always told us that he was happy that everything happened. He never really regarded our feelings for it. He never asked us how we felt.

**Amanda:** He painted a picture for me and my sister, like, You guys get to live with me, and everything's gonna be like all rainbows and butterflies. After the [yearlong] restraining order ended, he was telling us, "You see? "She's not even reaching out to you, she doesn't want to talk to you, she doesn't care about you. The restraining order is over, and she doesn't want to see you." So, I was like, Okay, well, if she doesn't want to see me, then why would I reach out to her? We kind of just stayed zero-contact and never communicated about the misunderstandings.

**Paige:** And then after that, we always told the court that we didn't want anything to do with my mom. We didn't want to go back to living with her. The reason we said this was because my father was constantly telling us to tell the court that. He said that if we were to say we live in an abusive household, then they were gonna send us away to foster care. So I always believed that, and he always made it seem like if we go to foster care, I'm never gonna see my parents again, and when we get to foster care, they're gonna separate my sister and me. So that would be even worse because, on top of being separated from my entire family, he also told us that we would be moving away to somewhere else. So we avoided saying anything at that point, at all costs. We just said whatever he told us to say.

As children, we didn't really question it; we kind of just went with whatever my dad said. And because I was saying these things, I felt guilty, like I was such a horrible child, a horrible daughter, because of me, because of my actions, my mom, my own mother, doesn't love me. There were several people that asked me, "What happened to your mom?" And I just basically told them what my dad put in my head: that my mom was very abusive toward us. I started to believe it. And that's what I would tell people, like my friends, "Oh yeah, my mother was abusive, so I don't live with her anymore." And after that, I didn't really go any deeper, and they didn't really ask that much either.

**Amanda:** I don't really remember watching my mom and my dad argue, but I feel like somewhere, like in the unconscious mind, it's definitely there.

**Paige:** From what I've heard, my father was very controlling towards my mother. He didn't allow her to have any guy friends and always asked her where she was. He even followed her everywhere when she wasn't aware of it. At the time, I only had visitations with him, so I never was able to see him do any of that. And then when I went to live with him, that's when he started being very controlling of my sister and I. He paid for our phones, so he always said that we had to answer his calls, his messages.

He would always ask us where we were going, who we were with. I was, I think, fifteen when I started going out with some friends, so I understand that part. But after a couple of years, I think after I turned eighteen, nineteen, twenty, he was still constantly calling me, controlling me, asking me who I was with, where am I going, and why am I taking so long? So the same behaviors that he was presenting towards my mother, he was doing towards me and my sister.

**Amanda:** He was texting me 24/7, calling me all day, every day, and I kind of grew up with it. I thought it was normal. I was like, oh well, he's checking up on me because he loves me, and since my mom doesn't do that, then she doesn't love me. By the time I went to live with him, it was already normalized. But he was never really physically present. He was always working. So he would call me. He called me to wake me up, to go to school. He called me before I left the house because I was walking. He called me when I got to school. He called me when I got out of school, and he called me when I got home. And when I got a job, he would call me when I got to work, on my lunch, when I got out of work, and then when I got home. I had to check in with him, and he knew the time spans—how far away my job was, how far away the school was, and what time I should be home.

**Paige:** My father was very neglectful, not just in the mental sense, but also in the physical sense. He never put any effort into getting us to school or home safely. He just kind of allowed us to do whatever we had to do. Nutrition was another issue. He didn't have any clue on how to take care of us. He kind of just threw whatever together and said, "Eat it or don't eat it." It got to the point where he didn't really care about what I ate, so he would just feed me whatever I wanted, and at the time, I had a problem with sugar, so he would just buy me cookies, brownies, whatever, and he'd be like, "Okay, you'll survive off of this." I didn't have any energy to do anything except just to stay home. So I didn't really exercise, and I barely had energy for school. I don't remember even trying to focus in school; I kind of just neglected it and went to work.

And, since he didn't provide us with the best food, it was up to us to find somewhere to eat. So we depended on fast food and restaurants, and would always eat out, and that obviously cost us money. And he wouldn't buy us clothes. So it was up to us to buy ourselves clothes, food, school supplies, things like that. My sister started working when she was fifteen, and I began working at sixteen. From a very young age, my father insisted on me getting a car and a license. He said, "Okay, you work so you can get your license, so you could pay for your own car." So, from a young age, I had the big responsibility of a car loan.

**Paige**: I felt as if my life wasn't even my own; I wasn't allowed to do anything for myself. Everything I was doing was for his approval in a way. He called us to wake us up when we left the house, when we got to school, when we got out of school, when we got home, and then, once we got home from school, he would be calling us several times just to ask what we were doing. So that was his way of controlling us, and if I ever went out with any friends, he would constantly call me.

**Amanda**: I thought it was normal, so I found a relationship like that. I attracted someone who was equally as toxic as my dad. That constant hyper-vigilance and negativity and threats and stuff depressed me. I was quarantined during the COVID-19 pandemic with both of them and was not allowed to have friends. If I had a friend, it was a problem. So these two people were the only people in my life.

**Paige**: It was very isolating. I didn't have any close friendships. It's kind of hard to make a friendship that goes that deep if I don't know myself that deeply.

**Amanda**: The only times I would think about my mom, I was hurt. I was pretty depressed and lonely, and this caused a lot of unhealthy attachment issues. I just thought, *Not even my mom loves me, so no one would love me. My dad's the only person who would be capable of loving someone like me.*

**Paige**: I didn't even really talk to my sister about it. At the time, we didn't have the skills to express our emotions. My father was very much like, "You have to deal with it, life is hard, that's it." He didn't really care about how we're supposed to feel. He didn't tell us, "You're supposed to feel sad, you're allowed to feel sad, let it out." It was very hard to be vulnerable, even to my father. I really thought that I could have trusted him, and I remember there was a time where I was hurting myself. I used to cut my arms, and when my father found out, he didn't really show any sense of care or concern. He was more like, "How can you do this?" He was *angry* with me for doing that. So that made me feel like no one really cared about how I felt or why I was doing what I was doing. It was more like what I was doing was wrong, and I should just stop. So that also made me neglect my own feelings. I didn't trust anybody at that point—not myself, not my sister, not my dad— and I also had a couple of therapists, and they never really went that deep either. When it came to him, I was always against what he was telling me. I would still do what he said, but I would always question it, and he didn't like that.

My sister, on the other hand, is more of a people pleaser, so she was always the one to go comfort him. My sister would be the one to go to him, like, "Oh, I'm sorry this happened, what can I do?" My father used that against her and kind of made her the, I guess, the wife role. My dad would not really do much, but my sister would clean, she would cook, she would just be there for him the way he wanted a wife, and since my sister didn't know any better, she just did whatever my father told her, because she basically thought that my father was this big person in her life, the only person that she has, and the only person that really loves her. That's what he made it out to be: that he's the only person who loves my sister and me as well. So obviously my sister wanted to protect him.

**Amanda:** I would watch videos on how to build a child's confidence, and it's basically like you have to let them do things on their own and make mistakes, and find out and learn from them. But my dad, if I made a mistake, then it was the worst thing ever, and I was a horrible person. So I never really did anything because I didn't want to make a mistake. I was scared to make my own decisions. So I just kind of grew up not making decisions. I was kind of like, *oh well, if he wants me to do this, then I'm gonna do this because this is what he wants.* And if I were to think otherwise, then there's gonna be conflict, and I didn't want conflict because I was a people pleaser.

Something that changed was that I started going to therapy when I was seventeen years old. At this point, I had been going to therapy ever since I was four. I had had five therapists, and I never took it seriously because I was always like, *oh well, I can't talk about this, so I'm not gonna talk about it.* So we never got anywhere. But by the time I was seventeen, I went to therapy because I was put in a situation in a relationship. This relationship started when I was fourteen, and it just made everything worse; it made my depression a lot worse.

**Paige:** Before he met my mother, [my dad] had a wife and two other children. So after it didn't work out with the mother of his first kids, he tried to have his first kids with him, but they left to their mother's side of the family. So that's when he had that visitation with my sister and me; he was holding on to us. It didn't work out with the mother of his first children, and so this has happened before; he already tried to take them away from their mother, too, really.

Getting reconnected with my mom actually started very randomly. My sister turned eighteen, and she got a tattoo. My dad went crazy because of that, and my sister was like, *I wonder how my mom would react if I got a tattoo.* So that's when we started to wonder what she's up to and what life would be like if we lived with her instead.

My sister reached out to my mom. They met up and talked, and my mom shared her experience with my father. That made my sister feel validated, because my sister did not feel safe with my father and didn't understand why. When my mom explained her situation, my sister felt understood. It was kind of as if the blindfold was ripped off: my father has been this way the entire time.

My sister needed time to think, but my father threatened to kill himself if she didn't come back. I took him to the hospital. He had to stay there, and I was alone because my sister still needed time apart. It was a very dark time in my life. And that's when my mother came in and opened her apartment to me. She said, "You can come to me if you need me; I'm there for you." This entire thing just happened with my father, and my mother was still there to welcome me with open arms. So that was when I felt like, *okay, my mother really does love me.* Even after everything, even after all this time we spent apart, she welcomed me with open arms and she was there for me.

So that was what did it. That was what made me realize, *okay, my mother doesn't hate me like I thought.* Ever since then, I've always worked to build a relationship with her. Obviously, it's very difficult; it took a lot of healing and understanding between all of us, and yes, we all have to do our part, but it really is worth it in the end.

**Amanda:** I was just taking a look at a picture of my mom and realizing that, *oh, she's been here; she didn't leave; she does want us in her life.* That was when we started living with my mom again. And ever since then, it's been difficult, because she has the resentment of everything that happened years ago. I have the resentment that *you* chose to leave and you weren't there for me, like you never reached back out. Right now, it has been pretty difficult because we're still both hurt over everything that happened.

**Lisa:** Suppose I have a twelve-year-old who needs help, whose behavior is like your dad's. How can I help?

**Paige:** First, I would definitely say just listen to her. Maybe try to explain to her what her father is like, because as a child, you wouldn't really understand. They're not going to see that there's anything wrong with their parent. So I would just try to explain to them that he might not be a bad person, but he could definitely be manipulating her. If you try to avoid telling them, that's just gonna make them believe the other parent even more. It's tricky. I felt like if I said the wrong thing, someone was gonna turn on me. If I had a parent who would listen to me with absolutely no judgment, I would definitely feel more open to talking about how I felt and what's going on around me.

**Amanda:** I grew up with a lot of guilt and shame, as if I deserved everything that happened. I don't know about every parent, but I would say not to make the child feel more guilty for leaving; don't make them feel guilty when they're back in your presence because it's just making things harder, it's making them more uncomfortable to hear about how you chose to leave.

A wall was built up for me to not really feel comfortable enough to communicate my true thoughts to my mom, because I was like, okay, well, you have this idea of the situation, and you're not willing to listen about what actually happened, and your idea is fixed. So it's really hard for me to get a word in without there being conflict.

So I would say to just be open-minded and listen to everything that is, even if it hurts to hear, even if it doesn't align with what you think the situation is. Just listen, just let them speak, give them a safe space to just talk.

**Paige:** There's definitely hope. You can't just give up completely, because there's always hope. I never expected to see my mom again. I kind of had to live with the fact that all this happened, and I already, at that point, accepted the fact that I was never going to see my mom again, and she was going to hate me forever. But then, plot twist, I spoke to my mom out of nowhere, kind of randomly, and now we've been living together for almost a year, and our relationship is thriving.

It took a lot of work, of course, but it really is worth it. I know it's very difficult to have your child not want to speak to you, and they don't want to put in the effort. I would definitely say be understanding of that and just be there for them when they are ready, because they might not even understand. You can show them that you love them by listening, being there for them, and allowing them to come back at their own pace.

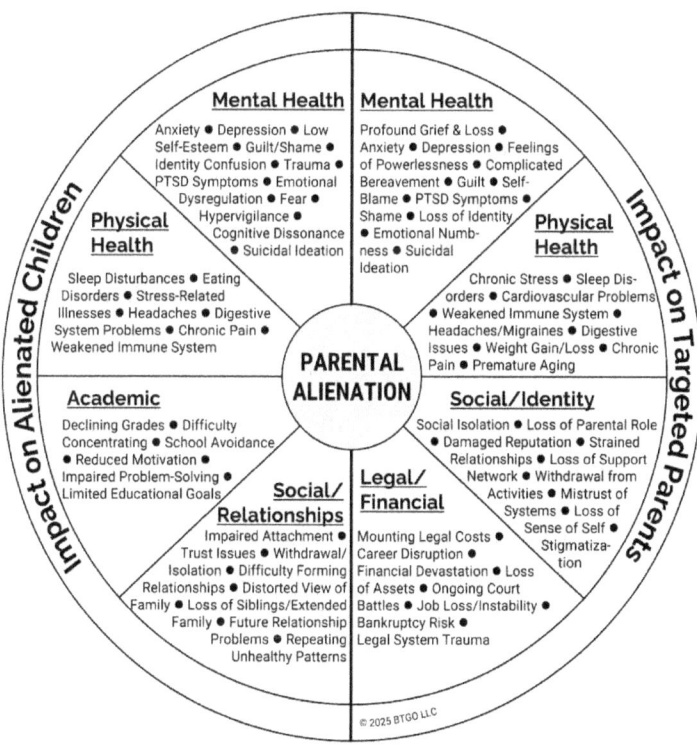

## Long-Term Effects

If alienation is happening, realize that you are not the primary victim; your child is. And the effects of parental alienation are not something that they'll "just grow out of." To the contrary, the impact will likely show up in different ways throughout their lives, and they'll have a lot more than the normal emotional baggage we all carry around with us. How alienation in childhood affects adults remains a relatively under-researched topic, but the research that exists is consistent. One study found that adults exposed to parental interference and alienation as children display:

1. Lower self-esteem and self-sufficiency.
2. Higher alcohol and drug use rates.
3. Parental relationship difficulties.
4. Insecure attachment.
5. Lower quality of life.
6. Higher divorce rates.
7. Feelings of loss, abandonment, and guilt.
8. Depression and anxiety symptoms, including empty depression, where a person lacks a clear identity because they never individuated developmentally.
9. Repetition of these alienating behaviors on their children by their partner or their own children's grandparents.

If the quantity or quality of your parenting time is being taken from you by an alienating co-parent, we suspect that you'd learn to deal if you could only know that your kids would be OK. The evidence says otherwise. Alienation is a form of child abuse, and your children are at serious risk of lifelong problems if something isn't done to counter the impact.

## Alienation-Proofing

How can our kids learn to have healthy relationships, making them less likely to be brainwashed? It starts with making sure they have a healthy relationship with us.

Parenting coach Mike Barsamian has observed that when our kids become teens, everything seems to center on logistics. When's the track meet? Whose house are you going to? When do you need me to pick you up from school?

Connecting with our kids relies on much more than surface engagement, and this part is going to take some real work. Barsamian says that understanding the nuance of the following three things can change the way you perceive and strengthen the foundation of your relationships with your kids:

1. **Consideration.** A considerate person is somebody who wants to understand you and cares about what's meaningful to you. In relationships, when somebody is considerate, they're growing in their understanding of who you are now, and who you're becoming as you grow throughout life.

2. **Appreciation versus Admiration.** Barsamian calls appreciation "oxygen for the soul," or valuing somebody for who they are. *Admiration* instead values someone for what they *do*. This is where parents can get confused.

   Your kid says, "I'm getting an A!" You reply, "Nice job! You get a reward." That dynamic is a common one, and there's nothing wrong with it, but giving admiration to our kids doesn't improve our relationships because it is performance-based. Admiration is nice, but what fills our cup is appreciation.

Many people never feel truly appreciated in their relationships, and that's because we don't pay attention. We're busy, and we get distracted. It takes effort to be present so that we can radiate appreciation.

Try to intercept performance-driven messages like, "Hey, thanks for cleaning the house." Instead, try something like, "I appreciate the way that you helped me out around the house this weekend...we got everything cleaned up!" Or, "What I really appreciate is how kind you are, and that you took the time to help me do something important."

Hear the difference?

3. **Communication.** It is the final element to ensure you and your kids stay connected.

**Barsamian suggests examining yourself first and understanding how you relate to your child before looking at them and criticizing.** The hard part is usually taking the time to slow down and look through those three lenses of consideration, appreciation, and communication. How are *you* doing? How are *you* showing up?

## Questions for Reflection

1. What do you appreciate about your child, and how do you show your appreciation? When's the last time you showed it?
2. What can you do to show consideration towards your child? Is it taking them out to dinner at their favorite restaurant? A small gift? Taking a little more time to listen? How have you been considerate of your kid in the past two weeks?

3. How can you acknowledge your child's stress? Saying something like, I know you're working hard right now. What can I do to help you? Not making them do chores for a day because you recognize that they have exams?

## CHAPTER 3

# A DISTORTED VIEW OF REALITY: WHY THEY DO IT

*"I'm going to leave you bleeding in the street, on your knees, begging me for mercy."*

—Our client's ex, to our client

**Your Own Personal Terrorist**

When your relationship with a toxic partner ends, their desire to exert power over you does not. Under the same roof, they had plenty of ways to get to you. Once separated, however, their avenues are limited to three big areas: money, court, and, worst of all, your kids. They concentrate their efforts here, and our clients who have bled money in the legal system, dealing with motion after motion, know deeply how hard this is.

If you can't be controlled, you must be destroyed…completely. But weaponizing your children is a whole new level, where the harm doesn't come to just you. When the conflict never ends, and your ex can't let go, kids get pulled into the fray with terrible effect, as we saw in Chapter 2. When it rises to the level of alienation, the damage can be devastating. So, why in the world would someone do this?

## Anger That Does Not Subside

Did you ever notice, when you were in the relationship, that your ex held grudges against many people, both past and present? That their list of those who had wronged them was a long one? Well, congratulations: you're now on it. They will never "forgive" you, and it is likely that the co-parenting relationship will be a search for ways to manipulate the situation to continue their power game. We see this every single day in our work with our clients and the broader community. So, no, you're not imagining it, and it's quite possible that there's more going on than you realize.

We'll dive deeper into the motivations, but it comes down to one overriding reason that they do this: their anger with you for… well…everything…never subsides. You now have your own personal terrorist.

## Five Big Triggers

People like your ex tend to have an all-or-nothing attitude. They think that everyone is either all good or all bad. Of course, you're all bad, so anything is justified. They'll create any story they can to legitimize your destruction. Divorce is one of the emotionally rawest times for everyone, but especially so for a personality-disordered ex. Alienation coach Charlie McCready notes five big triggers that might set someone like your ex off:

1. **Separation.** The end of the relationship triggers feelings of abandonment for your ex. When you split, they vilify you because you've destroyed the facade of a wonderful life that they were presenting to the world. They detest you because you've removed a comfort blanket that was

used as a crutch for them; they don't want you to be with anyone else, and that includes your own children.

2. **Anything to do with the court.** Any legal event—a mediation date, a new filing, an appearance—is an inflection point that may put your ex on full alert during these times, actively looking for opportunities to attack. Might they present new false accusations? Absolutely. Attempt to distract from important issues? For sure! Because they are so ungrounded in reality and convinced that they deserve 100% of everything, it is also very hard to negotiate with an abusive ex, which is why many of these cases do end up in court, putting decision-making into the hands of a stranger. This takes away everyone's control and may leave your ex feeling extremely vulnerable, which is why we often see a spike in their terrorist activities, like lashing out at you with a steady stream of nasty messages.

3. **Money.** What's mine is mine, and what's yours is mine too. In their view, they are entitled to whatever they want. Keep in mind that narcissists and other toxic personality types frequently get a boost to their precarious self-esteem from material things, not relationships. Money and other signs of wealth are status symbols that prop them up. Anything that hits your ex in the wallet is a hot button.

4. **Your positive relationship with your child.** Your ex's narrative is that any good relationship you have with your child is fake, and so they'll also do whatever it takes to ruin it, either in reality or public perception. Since you were blamed for the problems in the relationship and

were certainly the cause of its demise, any sign that you get along just fine with your child is a threat.
5. **Your new relationship.** When you move on to a new, healthy relationship, your ex will spin a version of reality that fits their narrative—that either your new partner must be "fooled" by not yet realizing what a monster you are, or that anyone who cares for you must be a demon. The real message is one of envy: How dare YOU be happy?

Brace yourself for the venom that will come at your new partner from your ex to undermine their relationship with your child as well.

Studies show that many people who encourage their children to reject the other parent do so to exact revenge, obtain an ally, or to cope with loneliness or jealousy. Some trick themselves into believing they're doing what's best for the kids because they convince themselves that the other parent is unsafe.

## No Solid Ground

Chris loves playing golf. He's decent at it, but far from great. If he plays a bad round and one of his buddies comments that he's not a good player, that doesn't send him into a tailspin. He knows it was a bad day, and that he'll have better days too. His perception is grounded in objective reality. He doesn't need the validation of others to feel okay about himself. With toxic people, something is broken. They don't have their own well-grounded reality. Because they can't feel it inherently, they require other people to satisfy their need to be validated and rely on the admiration and praise of others to support their self-esteem.

In our experience, these types of personalities have a series of core motivations that fuel their burning desire to destroy you, and in turn, their alienation campaign. At the center of everything is an inability to self-regulate. This hole needs to be filled, which manifests itself in a variety of ways:

### Need for Power and Control

Divorce represents a loss of control, and alienating your child becomes a way to reassert dominance over you in the new family dynamic. They believe that you're not entitled to a separate relationship with your child, because that would exist outside their control. So they try to dictate what your child thinks, how they feel, and who they love.

### Fear of Being Replaced

The separation itself has already triggered feelings of abandonment, and now they are terrified that your child might "choose" you over them. By "grooming" before the relationship ends, they make a preemptive strike at this perceived threat and try to ensure your kid's loyalty will rest only with them.

### Sense of Entitlement

Narcissistic parents often believe that the children "belong" to them. How dare you want to preserve your role as a parent?

### Black-and-White Thinking

Many people with personality disorders have a "you're with me or against me" attitude and see the world through extremes. People who love, admire, and align with them are "good"; anyone who doesn't is "evil."

## Lack of Empathy

You probably realized at some point in your former relationship that your ex appeared unable to understand other people's feelings. Perhaps they seem concerned and interested in your children, but instead demonstrate a profound disregard for their emotional needs.

## Pathological Envy

Your ex feels entitled to your child's exclusive love and attention and resents any affection they display toward you or anyone associated with you. People like them often experience intense envy when they perceive that you have something they don't, such as a close relationship with your child.

## Vindictiveness

Their need for revenge manifests in a joy in seeing you suffer, and what better way to inflict pain than to take away the person you love the most?

In the context of our high-conflict co-parenting community, an alienating parent perceives themselves as entirely good and a victim, and you as entirely bad.

## A Distorted Reality

One of the biggest questions we get in our world is, Do they know what they're doing?

This is a complex, multi-layered topic. In the end, their behavior is harming your relationship with your child, and you need to deal with it. Their perception is so distorted that they genuinely believe that you're truly harmful as a parent, despite all the evidence to the contrary.

Remember that your ex does not share your value of putting the kids first. But brace yourself for claims that they alone are the empathic parent who is truly focused on what's best. Confronting them about their behavior just leads to projection, blame-shifting, and further entrenchment in their position. Logic simply does not apply unless it suits their needs.

We believe that indeed they are aware of what they're doing, but are so skilled at creating an alternate view of reality that they exist in a world where their actions are not only justified, but noble.

## Questions for Reflection

1. Which of the five triggers (separation, court events, money, your relationship with your child, your new relationship) seems to most consistently set off increased alienating behavior from your ex?
2. Thinking about your ex's core motivations (need for control, fear of being replaced, sense of entitlement), which seems to drive their behavior most?
3. How might understanding this help you respond more strategically?

# CHAPTER 4

# HOW IT BEGINS: PRE-ALIENATION AND POISONOUS MESSAGES

> *"The more your ex can have your child internalize disaffection for you, the less work [they] will have to do in isolating your child from you.",*
>
> —Dr. Amy Baker, Psychologist

## Grooming & Pre-Alienation

Narcissistic abuse recovery coach Jon McKenney remembers the first Father's Day after his divorce and not hearing a word from any of his four kids. He knew that the message they received from their mom was that if they didn't want to, they wouldn't have to talk to him, instead of the fact that he is, has been, and will remain their dad for the rest of their lives. Jon realized that his ex had discouraged the relationship long before their separation occurred. He recalls that during conversations about their impending divorce, his ex asserted that his kids would "never forgive you and will never want to be in touch with you."

Although Jon felt as though he had done everything to keep the marital issues separate from the children, he discovered that his ex had been trashing him for a decade before they actually separated. It felt like they all would "get into this little huddle together." His ex's distrust of him bled onto their children. There was a lot of triangulation going on, where his ex placed herself between Jon and other significant family members. Instead of the kids communicating with him directly, they would talk to their mother, who would relay information. The same thing happened with Jon's parents, who started speaking through her about their own family plans.

Healthy, mature people divorce all the time and do what they can to support the kids' relationship with both parents. Instead, Jon's ex sent the message to their children that he had abandoned the whole family.

### What is Pre-Alienation?

Bill Eddy is a conflict resolution expert, a former social worker and family law attorney, founder of the High-Conflict Institute, and author of more than twenty books, including *Don't Alienate the Kids*. With a high-conflict parent, Eddy says, children quickly learn who has power and who doesn't in the family. Being on the "winning side" is something that children may perceive as necessary for survival. Long before their parents' divorce, kids are already on a path toward being turned against several other people in their lives.

Alienation coach Charlie McCready coined the term "pre-alienation" to describe the behaviors that plant the seeds of a negative narrative to your kids, starting long before an actual separation. You may have realized that while still in the relationship, your ex made you the butt of jokes or found ways to undermine your authority. Lisa remembers when her son was in elementary school and how, when she would attempt to discipline him, her ex would say, "You don't have to listen to Mom —she's just cranky."

This kind of damage can be so subtle that you just may believe that it's part of normal family dynamics, that marriage is hard, or you imagine that this is just what happens when the romance is gone. What's really going on is that your ex is slowly laying the foundation to swoop in and take the kids. This premeditated, relentless attack against your character can go on for just a few months or several years, but it definitely escalates when an abusive ex believes that it's getting close to the end of your relationship.

**Hatred by Association**

Those closest to you are also affected. *Hatred by association* occurs when your kids want nothing to do with anyone associated with you. Relatives who have been close are suddenly discarded as well. Grandparents, aunts, uncles, and cousins may be harshly criticized and cut off.

One of our clients' parents had been very present in his children's lives, coming to every school event and all sports games. After separation, however, his children decided that they were "dangerous." You may feel pressure to defend innocent family members from your child's condemnation, but according to Dr. Kristin A. Roorbach, an educational psychologist specializing in pediatric trauma, the best thing to do is choose the side of your child, which can be tough when having to also take care of the emotional needs of loved ones that cannot understand why they too have been rejected.

Instead of pushing your child, Roorbach suggests telling your family, "It looks like they're not ready for you to give them a big hug right now, and we're trying to work things out." It can feel counterintuitive, but for the moment, your kids need the importance of their own feelings reinforced by you.

## Irreplaceable

New romantic relationships present a unique challenge. You can know with something approaching certainty that your new partner will be Public Enemy #1 from the moment your ex knows they exist.

When Maarit, co-founder of Blended Family Frappe, would join her husband at any of his children's activities, his ex would approach and start talking to him without even acknowledging her. Her stepdaughter followed her mother's lead without even saying hello, acting as though Maarit were invisible. She found the experience incredibly isolating, so she decided to skip her stepkids' events.

Many stepparents have to bear a lot. They may have household responsibilities, but don't enjoy any of the benefits of being a parental figure to your kids. Often they have strong feelings about what constitutes good parenting, but they're not in the position—situationally or legally—to have any power, or to even voice those opinions without causing more trouble.

Because your new partner doesn't have a deep, lifelong attachment to your child, they can become a much easier target for your ex. Children are often also dealing with lingering feelings of grief over their parents' divorce, and at the same time, they're being subjected to your ex's terror campaign. They may be unable or unwilling to allow a positive relationship to occur out of fear of being disloyal. It's a tough spot to be in.

Under the influence of a toxic co-parent's alienation campaign, the kids will often resent your new partner. If you do start a new relationship, you want to avoid pressuring them to feel obligated to have a particular relationship with him or her. As psychologist Dr. Josh Coleman says, "you chose the new partner; your kids didn't. They shouldn't have to deal with expectations that they'll accept them as a near-parent. Your partner can certainly gain a big role in your kids' lives, but let it be on your children's timeline."

## "You Love Your New Partner More Than Me!"

Toxic exes create no-win situations, especially when you get romantically involved with someone else. They may encourage your already highly sensitive children to believe that there must not be enough love and attention to go around, which becomes fertile ground for them to also paint you as unloving and unavailable.

This was something that our friend, grief therapist and author Jessica Anne Pressler, experienced in her former marriage. Her then-husband's ex suggested to their daughter that her father did not love her enough, and his daughter demanded that he choose between her and Jessica. Her husband did not recognize the dynamic, but of course did not want to risk the possible loss of his daughter, and this thorny issue was part of what led to the demise of their relationship.

However, if your ex becomes involved with someone new, that's an entirely different story. Here, they may instead scorn you to the children, saying that you stayed single because you're not worthy enough to find someone else.

## You Don't Always Need to Make Nice

Traditional co-parenting advice suggests that everyone put their differences aside and maybe even sit together at children's events. That doesn't work in our world, can be very difficult for someone who can't stand hypocrisy, and isn't the best for anyone's mental health—especially children's—in situations like these. Maarit says it was exasperating to be expected to "put on your party manners" with so much litigation and war going on behind the scenes.

Behavioral analyst Theresa Inman echoes that children sense when there's hostility, and that you don't want them growing up thinking it's ok to pretend to be perfect in public and act as though everything is fine when behind closed doors it's a very different scene.

A better approach is to support your child and give them the option to sit wherever they want. And, critically important, don't let them see if their choice hurts your feelings.

## Their Tactics

In our work with our coaching clients, we prioritize a deep understanding of what parental alienation is and how it's treated by the courts in custody cases, and focus on these two perspectives:

1. How to strategically communicate with your ex to build a legal argument for a custody case if your ex is engaging in alienating behaviors.
2. How to ensure that you are not doing anything that could be construed as alienating unconsciously, to insulate you against false claims of alienation by your ex.

Dr. Amy Baker's excellent book *Co-Parenting with a Toxic Ex*, describes a number of alienating behaviors, the first of which is present in every case we've seen. We'll get into deeper detail on this foundational element for the remainder of this chapter.

## Sending Poisonous Messages About the Other Parent

Toxic parents often try to erode the healthy, natural bond that has existed between you and your child since birth. They want your child to believe that you are unsafe, unloving, or unavailable. It rarely starts with obvious lines, like "Your mother is a bad person."

The initial messages are usually way more subtle, and children aren't mature enough to recognize them. You correct your child for some minor transgression, and your ex rolls their eyes. You meet for an exchange as your ex is dropping your child off, and while hugging them goodbye, your ex stage whispers, "Call me any time if you don't feel safe."

An alienating parent constantly speaks negatively about the other parent to the child in a way that matches how far it has progressed, subtle at first, and more overt in time, as their campaign gains traction and the wedge between you and your child is driven deeper. This can include direct insults, accusations, spreading rumors, and exaggerating minor flaws or incidents. Their goal is to create a negative image of you in your child's mind.

### Ground Zero: The Early Stages of Divorce or Separation

No matter how angry or resentful you feel towards your ex, it's important to remember that anything bad you say about them to your kid will be internalized unconsciously as a criticism. A child perceives that they are part of both of you. Supporting the child's relationship with the other parent should be a shared goal, and is also one of the most important behaviors courts look for in custody cases. Healthy parents make a sincere attempt to shield children from negative emotions towards their ex, and want to help them get through this difficult time as unscathed as possible. Not so with your toxic ex. They draw the children into a "package deal" of victimhood, with the idea that only **you** did this to **them**. It's an easy extension of the narcissist's sense of abandonment.

Divorce is generally due to complex issues between two adults, but your ex's message may be, "or, "I had to leave your dad to keep you safe." The situation is ripe for blame, and a toxic ex is eager to point the finger at you, regardless of who actually made the decision to leave. These messages flourish during the upheaval of a new breakup, when children have their world rocked by the explosion of the family unit as they knew it. This is a difficult time for everyone, and children tend to wish more than anything else that their parents would get back together.

**Diminishing Your Love**

Your strong bond with your child is threatening to an emotionally unhealthy co-parent who views themselves as all good and you as all bad. This does not leave room for your child to love both of you. Your ex may try to invalidate your child's love for you by sending messages that your own love for your kids is insincere. If your child expresses affection for you, it will trigger them. This is when they will attempt to create suspicion, and either remind the child of something negative about you, or make a comment like, "It's good to see Mom/Dad finally being nice to you."

If you've ever seen the award-winning movie, *The Whale*, actor Brendan Fraser's character depicts a father whose daughter grew up believing that her father didn't want her in his life. It is an excellent illustration of what this kind of emotional manipulation does, not only to a child, but to an entire family.

**Loyalty Conflicts**

During a separation, kids often feel like they have to pick sides, which can create something called *loyalty conflicts*. This is when someone has to choose between two people because of the antagonism they have toward each other. It's the same "black-and-white thinking" we associate with personality-disordered people, and a toxic ex will exacerbate the situation. You're with me or against me, so if you really love me, then you need to hate and or discard your other parent.

Children can easily be misled because a counter-parent, which is the word we use to describe what your ex does, will often take a grain of truth and wrap it in layers of lies and exaggeration (just like they do in court pleadings). Kids are put in a position where they feel like they have to give you up to please their other parent. There's a whole system of invisible rewards and punishments.

**Pathological Alignment**

As time goes on, your ex's goal is to create alignment with the children against you. They'll make themself out to be the safe, loving, available parent, and fan the flames of rejection that the child feels for you. They'll minimize the child's need for two parents—"I'll make sure you're OK." They encourage negative thinking about you, and because children usually have some instinctive sense that your ex's love is conditional, they find appeasement the easier path to a more comfortable life. They'll learn how to say and do what your ex wants because being around them is then so much easier to navigate. Remember that dynamic—walking on eggshells—from your own relationship?

In time, kids can absorb messages to such an extent that they become their own, as they quickly come to understand that expressing negative emotions towards you will be rewarded, and positive expressions will elicit displeasure or anger.

**Involving Kids in Conflict**

Another basic tenet of divorce is that keeping kids out of the conflict during and after a split is of paramount importance. Children shouldn't know about custody battles or parenting disagreements. A toxic parent will inappropriately share details of legal actions, often painting a picture to your child that you're trying to harm them in court.

During their two-year divorce, one of our clients' exes confided in their three children more details than he should have, leading them to believe that their mother had abandoned them by initiating the divorce. Every time she would show up for parenting time, the kids would stand in the doorway within earshot of their father and ask her to go through the details of what happened, and "address their concerns" before talking about anything else. They also insisted that she needed to spend her parenting time with them in the marital home while their father was there, and, after accepting gifts from her on Christmas, would subsequently return them.

**Using Children as Messengers**

Once the kids have come to view your ex as the victim of your cruelty, why not enlist them? They may be used to bring messages appealing to your kindness, cooperation, and mercy, as your ex enthusiastically throws you under the bus. One of our clients told us how her son said that his father told him that they were unable to take a planned vacation to Mexico because she "was keeping Dad in court."

What choice do you have? Do you correct the misinformation they've been fed, thus deepening their involvement in the conflict you're earnestly trying to keep them out of? Do you defend yourself? Do you take the "high road" in a continued attempt to keep them out of the fray, but risk intensifying their doubts about you?

**Weaponized Parenting Responsibilities**

Kids have a lot going on between school, extracurricular activities, haircuts, doctor appointments, and their social lives. And parenting as a single parent, especially when you have multiple children, can be a lot to manage. In a normal co-parenting relationship, people work together and help each other out with the kids. This, unfortunately, is not in the cards for you. With a difficult ex, when you're unavailable to jump when they want you to, don't be surprised that the message to the kids becomes that you don't value them enough to make time for them. "See? I'm always there for you; I'm sorry Mom/Dad doesn't feel the same way."

## Extracurricular Activities as a Trojan Horse

Normal parents encourage their children to get involved in extracurricular activities or sports, so they can remain active as well as socialize. But in some situations, the time spent doing things your kids enjoy can be used to whittle your parenting time away.

According to Maarit, extracurricular activities can sometimes be a Trojan horse for alienation. She and her husband lived far from his ex, and followed a long-distance schedule, where the kids stayed with their mother primarily during the school year, and with their father during the summers. Her stepdaughter got into competitive swimming, and without any shared discussion with her dad or herself, her mom told her daughter she could sign up for the swim team in their hometown. After the fact, she told Maarit and her husband that their daughter would be "so disappointed if you say no." This decision ended up having a significant impact on her husband's time with his daughter because the team met early every morning, and suddenly, he saw her a lot less frequently: He lost an entire summer with her, and during the school year, there were always more excuses. His ex signed their daughter up for several after-school enrichment activities, which continued to create more excuses to keep him from spending time with her.

Their daughter was constantly put in the middle. When her dad tried to get together with her, his ex would say that if she didn't go to practice, she would be "letting the team down because they expected her to be there." It turned into, "Well, your dad doesn't really seem to care about what's important to you. And then, 'He doesn't know you the way that I know you,'" which started to drive a wedge into the parent-child relationship. As their daughter got older, they would argue that her father was losing many hours with her, and she was subjected to countless guilt trips. The solution for their family was not easy, but at some point, Maarit and her husband, while acknowledging how crucial a certain extracurricular activity was, sent the clear message that nothing was more important than family. When kids live far away, it's necessary to prioritize family time, because there's already so little of it. These decisions are certainly not easy.

**Borrowed Scenarios**

> *"I'm starting to get really uncomfortable around my own kid. When we were having dinner last night, she kept putting her hand on her hip and saying, 'That's insane!' just like my ex! She had this expression on her face that didn't even look like her; she's only six!"*
>
> —Been There Got Out client

Do you ever feel like your ex's words are coming out of your child's mouth? This is called a *borrowed scenario*. When kids use words or phrases that seem like they're not their own, especially when they are more advanced than their normal language, that's a strong indication that they're repeating things they've heard from your ex.

When one of Chris' sons was very young, there was a period of almost two years during which he kept missing elementary school due to "stomachaches." The doctors couldn't find anything physically wrong, and he was seeing a therapist, but his mother would still keep him home from school two or more days a week. Attendance was becoming a serious problem. At home with her, he basically played with devices or watched TV alone all day.

During Chris' parenting time, he tried to work on getting his son to school. But we know how kids in these situations can play both parents, and Chris' son would call his mother early in the morning just as Chris was trying to get him out the door. One day, while on the phone with his mother, he screamed down the stairs, "Dad, you have no empathy!" This was not the vocabulary of an eight-year-old.

## Channeling Messages

How often does your child come to you from your ex's house and start making comments you know they have heard from your ex? One thing we see often is a child criticizing a targeted parent with comments like, "Mom's right, you're really cheap because you don't pay for our school supplies," even when your agreement indicates that this is covered by child support. Or even more insidiously, "Dad says that you're the one who's not letting us go on vacation to Aruba," when your ex is constantly violating the parenting agreement with time grabs and putting the kids in the middle.

## The Rule Follower vs. the Fun Parent

Kids love, at least superficially, an environment where they can have cookies with breakfast, stay up as late as they want, neglect their homework, and be on devices constantly, even if these things are terrible for their growth and development. An alienating parent often tries to win their loyalty by having fewer restrictions.

Does your ex offer your teenager greater freedom, with less discipline? This is something we see all the time. When a child perceives that one parent gives them more privileges, making them feel more trustworthy or mature, they prefer to spend time with that parent. In the meantime, the parent doing the discipline and drudgery can look like "the bad guy."

With brains that are not fully developed, children don't have the emotional maturity to recognize what's good for them, and an alienating parent who initiates a popularity contest puts you in a terrible position. At the same time, your kid may have a fear-based relationship with your ex and may, ironically, align with a harmful parent because they're trying to appease them. According to Charlie McCready, the child is in "damage mitigation" mode because they want the least amount of pain.

### Impact on the Targeted Parent

We don't need to tell you that alienation isn't very good for your own mental or physical health. The most common emotions those in our community express are rage, injustice, and a heartbreaking sense of loss over the missing presence of a child who is often tantalizingly close. The entire problem is the wedge that your ex is intentionally driving between you. Targeted parents are frequently overcome with guilt for feeling unable to do anything.

From a practical standpoint, we see that people are under such distress that the emotional impact alone can feel paralyzing; getting unstuck enough to try to fix the root problem can seem unimaginable. We're big believers in the mind-body connection, and many of our clients have dealt with physical effects ranging from weight gain or loss, insomnia, and fatigue, to ailments including autoimmune disorders and cancer as a result. They may develop unhealthy coping strategies as well, including substance abuse. Research shows that alienated parents show increased incidence of suicide attempts.

If you don't have a therapist with the right skill set, not only does it not help, but you can lose confidence, in turn potentially harming your recovery and mental health overall. How awful to have your ex take away so much from you—even your very sense of self —and then have their impact outlast the relationship itself.

## Questions for Reflection

1. Looking back at your relationship before separation, what examples of "pre-alienation" behavior can you now identify? Think about times your ex undermined your authority, made you the butt of jokes, or sent subtle messages that you were the problem parent.

2. Which specific poisonous messages is your ex sending about you being unsafe, unloving, and/or unavailable?

3. How has *hatred by association* affected your child's relationships with your family members, friends, or new partner?

# CHAPTER 5

# THE TENTACLES OF POISON

> "Since the divorce, my oldest hasn't talked to me in four years, and now his younger sister is starting to pull away. I'm terrified that I'm going to lose both of them."
>
> —Been There Got Out client

## Chronic Injustice

Children are hardwired to protect themselves. When one parent dominates the other, they may view that parent as the only one who can give them what they need. As we discussed in Chapter 1, a child is wired to attach to both parents. But when alienation occurs, they idealize one and develop contempt for the other. When asked why they hate you, they'll offer senseless comments like, "You don't smell good," or "You didn't let me have a doughnut for dinner." Attachment expert Dawn Brauer explains that this is about brainwashing, and what makes it worse is that your children may actually believe they're making healthy, independent decisions by not being around you, even if they can't articulate why.

Brauer uses the term *chronic injustice* to describe how frustrating this can feel because there's no logical reason why your child is pulling away. As time goes on, you might feel like the dynamic is devolving into the same one that characterized your relationship with your ex, where you're doing anything to avoid confrontations *with your own children*. While poisonous messages are the foundation of alienation, your ex's tactics go much deeper. In Chapter 1, we just scratched the surface of the alienation factors. Let's now explore the rest of them in more detail.

## Interfering with Contact & Communication

You can do a lot to combat your ex's alienation campaign through your own parenting, but you need the opportunity to actually be a parent. You need time with the kids or at least some degree of contact. You need opportunities to send healthy messages to contrast the narrative they're getting from your ex. Whether you have the majority of parenting time, every other weekend, or even less, as long as you have any contact at all, it's an opportunity to strengthen (or restore, if things have degraded substantially) your bond with your child. Your ex knows this on some level and sees your contact as a threat; they'll use dirty tricks to interfere.

## Time Grabs & Chipping Away at Your Influence

Be on the lookout for your ex to take away whatever access they can from you. Maybe they'll argue that it's "just easier" for them to take the kids to activities on your time, claim a child is "too sick" to see you, or conveniently do the school pickup… and keep them through dinner.

Over time, you'll probably find that any deviations from the schedule always seem to go in one direction—more time for them, and less for you. Don't fool yourself into thinking that this isn't intentional and will somehow balance out. If you assert yourself and resist their attempts to eat away at your time, you're "rigid," unable to "co-parent cooperatively," and not doing what's "in the best interests of the children." They definitely won't comply with any "right of first refusal" that you might have in your parenting plan about your having the kids if they are unable to take care of them (those are notoriously hard to enforce). In the worst cases, they'll blatantly violate the schedule stipulated in your agreement or court order.

Yes, your parenting plan is a binding legal document that, at least in theory, you are both obligated to follow. But how do you enforce it? Many turn to the police, who dread domestic disputes because they can be so volatile. While a violation of a parenting schedule isn't exactly a domestic dispute, it does fall under the same umbrella, and police are often reluctant to get involved beyond logging a report (still a good idea).

It's disappointing just to be told to file something with the court for enforcement, although that may become necessary. It's critical to enforce your orders if your ex is violating them, and we'll get into how in Chapter 8. But at what point do you take that step? It can be a difficult decision, given how traumatizing court may have been in the past.

### Involving Kids in Deciding the Schedule

Enforcing your parenting time can be especially difficult with older children. Once kids get to the tween years, they crave agency in their lives. Your ex will feed on this and inappropriately invite them to have a say in the schedule, putting them squarely in the middle. Your ex might also position it as more of a "guideline" than a firm agreement, and paint you as entirely inflexible to your kids.

You probably struggled to stand up to your scary, explosive ex, so what chance do your kids have? If their alienation campaign has made progress, your child has been conditioned, so the easiest path is for them to choose not to be with you, as that's the only way that they'll be able to avoid your ex's wrath.

## Interfering with Calls

Another way your ex will cut you off is through interference with phone or video calls. We have seen everything under the sun when it comes to this. Alienating parents will completely miss scheduled calls with younger children, claiming they're "busy" with some important activity. They'll cut calls short. They might even block your number on kids' phones.

If your calls are scheduled, expect your ex to have the kids doing something fun during that time. Your contact then becomes a chore that takes them away from things they enjoy. Your ex may often try to communicate directly with you during these calls as well, causing your child confusion and discomfort.

## Monitoring Conversations

If you can't be prevented from having calls with your child, they'll try the next best thing: making sure you have no privacy, no way to connect authentically. They might talk to your child at the same time, distracting them, or you might hear them in the background, suggesting things for your child to say. When being monitored, your child can't feel safe expressing affection toward you openly, as they already know your ex will make life unpleasant as soon as they hang up.

This can happen in person as well. One of our clients' exes had violated their parenting plan for nine months, and the kids were being rewarded for not seeing their father. In this case, the alienation was advanced; our client had almost no contact. Not knowing what else to do, he would go to his ex's home to talk with them, and the kids insisted that any conversations take place within earshot of their mother.

Dr. Kristin Roorbach suggests a potential solution, recommending that you focus your attention on your child's feelings and approach from a perspective of curiosity. Start with something like, "If that's how you feel comfortable talking to me, I would be happy to talk with you there. But I'm actually curious as to why." Why tolerate a child dictating the terms of their contact with you? When things have deteriorated to this point, your first priority is digging out of the hole, says Roorbach, and making improvements, no matter how tiny and incremental.

So do what you can to keep the conversation going, remaining curious and asking for feedback. Remember that your child doesn't have a valid reason for severing their connection to you, but you don't want to pressure them into solving everything at once. "If you only want to talk to me here because you don't feel safe around me, what if we talk about ways that I could make you feel more comfortable? If it's because this home is what feels safe and comfortable, I understand, and let's talk about that. But if it's because you want (your other parent) to hear our conversation, then I would invite everybody to sit down right here."

To be strong enough to try this, you'll need to have done your own work so that you can be in the mental state to hold space for your children. Roorbach points out that this takes a lot of courage, and in order to be this courageous, you have to be grounded (and of course, in cases involving the potential for physical violence, getting together in person is not an option).

**Moving Away**

In extreme cases, a toxic parent may relocate to another area—with or without the court's approval—making the visitation schedule impractical or even impossible. In many jurisdictions, residency in a new location becomes permanent after six months, so it's especially important to act swiftly on any attempted move. Don't believe them for a moment when they say they need to go stay somewhere else with your child temporarily, and that they plan to come back!

**Erasing & Replacing**

Alienation is about diminishing you. Your ex is the only "real" parent (Chris' ex actually used these exact words), and thus the only one who matters. They will take steps to reprogram your children so that their wonderful memories of you as a parent don't reinforce your relationship with them.

Attorney Charles Jamieson says that most people erroneously believe that memory is like a videotape that remains unchanged. Instead, it is an active process, subject to distortion. When you have a child whose parent is being demonized, it's easy for that child's memory to be altered.

**Rewriting History**

In the later years of Chris' marriage, his ex was often out in the evenings, and during the work week, he was the one to manage the bedtime routine. The most wonderful part of that was story time. Reading with his sons at bedtime remains one of Chris' favorite memories of parenting when his boys were younger.

Years after his divorce was settled, Chris got a request from his ex that was…odd. She wanted a lot of the children's books in their extensive library. Never mind that their boys had long ago outgrown these books, and that they'd probably only become important again to them later on in life when reminiscing about their own childhoods.

By this time, Chris was able to figure out that she actually wanted the books so she could rewire their boys' memories to a fictitious past where she was the one who read them stories. She needed to erase, or at least minimize, a foundational connection their sons had with their dad.

## Blocking Your Access to Information

Your ex doesn't want any new history involving you, either. Your ongoing involvement with your child's education, therapy, or medical treatment is anathema to them, so they will look to obstruct you however they can. You might find that they have removed your name from school and doctor records, sometimes replacing it with their new partner's. Maybe your kids are on your ex's insurance, and they're claiming they can't figure out how to give you access to medical information. The pediatrician's office may not be willing to speak with you until you straighten things out. Your ex is also likely to conduct a smear campaign at the school, so teachers and administrators look at you like a criminal when you walk into the building.

And let's not forget extracurricular activities. By leaving you off contact lists, maybe claiming that the Little League team only allows one contact, your ex is hoping to leave you out of the loop, uninformed about the schedule. Ideally, to them, you won't show up for games or performances, further powering their narrative that you don't really care.

If, for some reason, your child knows you can't access some important information portal, can't you just hear your ex saying to them, "I know it's inconvenient, but (Mom/Dad) isn't allowed to access this information for grown-up reasons." Imagine the impression that makes on a child! How it might introduce doubt and suspicion, without anything more needing to be said.

## Mommy

Another way that they trivialize you to your kids is by encouraging them to refer to their own new partner as "Mommy" or "Daddy," or some nickname that implies the same thing. If you see it happening, you should almost certainly call them out immediately and insist that they stop. And be absolutely certain to never do this yourself. Courts frown on it, as it's terribly confusing for children. To your ex, you were always disposable. You could be easily swapped out for someone else, and when they find your replacement, they'll encourage your kids to replace you, too. Even if your ex has legally remarried, the two of you are your children's parents, and in most cases, you're the only ones with legal rights to act as such.

## Encouraging Your Child to Betray Your Trust

When your relationship with your ex ends, they lose most of their access to what's going on in your life. But when you're sharing physical custody, they have a ready-made solution, and will encourage the kids to be spies, whether reluctant ones or, in cases of more severe alienation, enthusiastic members of their intelligence team.

## Little Moles

Alienating parents commonly interrogate children as they go back and forth between their homes. They will grill them for all kinds of details about what went on during your time together. They might also be asking your child to go through your stuff, which could include your laptop, phone, or even dresser drawers. Don't leave anything that could be twisted into something incriminating where your ex's operatives could find it!

One of our clients' exes recruited their kids to go into his house and take photographs of his living space. When they passed the pictures to their mother, she labeled his residence "unlivable," and threatened to take him back to court for more custody. She rewarded the kids with video games when they behaved as her little spies. Our client felt like he had no privacy, and, worse, like he couldn't trust his own children.

Another problematic ex used recordings of arguments between their child and our client to file CPS complaints, trying to paint her as "unsafe." All of the cases were closed as "unfounded," but the impression created by a series of CPS investigations (where there's smoke, there's fire) can color a case. Beyond the constant fear that you'll "get in big trouble" when your ex twists something, your worries about your own children working as agents for the enemy erode the quality of your time with them. Your ex, in their twisted world, sees that as a fringe benefit.

**Shutting it Down**

Insisting your child not report back to your ex puts them in the middle of your conflict as collateral damage, which is exactly what your counter-parent is doing. We have to remember that although our kids are going through their own trauma, this doesn't mean that we shouldn't have rules and expectations.

According to child development expert AJ Gajjar, you must be mindful that "everything the child is experiencing with you has the potential to be reported back." So if there's anything in your home that you don't want them to see or know about, secure it and make sure the kids can't overhear private conversations.

This is more strategic than directly telling a child to stop their traitorous behavior. It's appropriate to say, "This is not okay," or "I don't appreciate that," and have a conversation about boundaries, which can help strengthen your relationship. It could also be a chance to encourage children to develop critical thinking skills and understand that they have a choice about how to behave. It isn't just, "Mom/Dad says to do it, so I have to do it." This is an opportunity to reflect with your child—how would they feel in your shoes?

Irish play therapist Edel Lawlor, who has worked with kids in the domestic violence space for decades, says that children have told her time and time again that they hate being grilled by either parent because they don't want to be involved in the conflict. A child candidly told Lawlor, "Sometimes I just say what she wants to hear: 'I had an awful time.' But I actually didn't. I had a great time."

What Lawlor recommends instead is that you do your best to stay completely regulated, so your child is comfortable enough to say that they miss the other parent, without fear that they will be hurting you.

## Undermining Your Authority

When your ex is able to establish their role as the only true authority—something they may have been laying the foundation for since before you split—you become greatly diminished in the eyes of your child, who may feel that your ex's power is universal.

- "Dad said you have anger issues, and I don't have to listen to you."
- "Mom says I need to go to bed at 8 p.m. at your house, too."
- "Dad doesn't want me to watch that movie without him."

When Lisa was still in her marriage and would discipline their son, her ex would tell him that he didn't have to listen, and would give him a way to "earn back" or otherwise undo whatever the consequence was. This totally undermined Lisa's ability to parent effectively and led to her son facing challenges in dealing with authority.

Years ago, not long after his marriage ended, Chris was dabbling in playing guitar. His older son played the upright bass in his school band, and his ex was also a music teacher. One Christmas, Chris thought it would be a lot of fun, and a great way to bond with his son, to get him an electric bass so they could play together. His son loved the gift, but months went by, and still it sat unused in the corner of Chris' living room.

When Chris finally asked him why he wasn't playing it, he answered that his mother had told him that he wasn't allowed to play until he had achieved certain proficiency goals with his classical bass.

What?

His ex had so effectively positioned herself as the sole authority that Chris' son left his gift unused without question. This brazen overreach served to undermine Chris on his own parenting time, destroyed a bonding opportunity, and turned any excitement their son had into another source of anxiety and disappointment. (We're happy to report that Chris' son now loves playing his electric bass!)

## Diminishing Your Parenting Role

Does disciplining your child feel impossible? One of the difficult things we have both experienced and witnessed in a number of our clients is when your child calls your ex to complain about your rules, and then your ex encourages them to ignore whatever they are.

When Chris' boys were much younger, one of them had an outburst right before a transition back to his mother, and among other things, dumped out the kitchen trash can on the floor as she pulled into the driveway. In his furor, he forgot to collect his backpack, which contained all his school things that would be needed the next morning, and stormed out of the house to his mother's waiting car. This was a golden opportunity for her. Shortly thereafter, still spun up, his son called Chris, demanding the backpack. Chris said that would be fine, but only after he cleaned up the mess he'd made, setting an effective boundary and reasonable conditions from a parenting standpoint. After being egged on by his mother, he came back to Chris' house and demanded to take the backpack without cleaning up. Chris stood firm on the condition that he pick up all the garbage first, but his son angrily refused and stomped out of the house for a second time, again without the backpack.

In a healthy co-parenting scenario, the other parent might tell a child that they shouldn't have acted out, that they need to respect both parents' rules, and, at the very least, clean up the mess. A "normal" parent would be respectful of their co-parent's discipline.

Instead, Chris' ex called the police.

She sat in her car up the street watching (and probably recording) while a police officer asked Chris for the backpack. Not wishing to escalate things further, Chris handed it over, sighed, and turned his attention to cleaning up the kitchen himself. What kind of message did this send to his son? "If you misbehave at Dad's, I'll reward you. I'll even swoop in and call the police to get him in trouble!"

As parents, our position is that of a role model, not just a disciplinarian. Your ex will look to destroy your influence along with your authority by insulting your beliefs, trivializing your life experiences, questioning your parenting abilities, and tarnishing your values. It's all a concerted effort to marginalize you in your child's mind.

Legal decision-making is also an area where we see our clients' exes constantly seeking to undermine their authority. When someone enrolls a child in an extracurricular activity or chooses a medical treatment with no meaningful discussion, your child receives the message that what you think is irrelevant, and on a larger level, meaningless.

### My Child Calls Me "Andrew!"

What's more brazenly disrespectful than your child calling you by your first name instead of Mom or Dad? If your ex is encouraging them to address you by your first name, Dr. Amy Baker suggests you say something like, "One of my favorite things is being your parent. I would really appreciate it if you went back to calling me (Mom/Dad) and not by my first name." If they listen, say thanks and praise them for being so respectful. If they don't, try to ignore it for the time being, and then give them positive attention or some kind of reward, if and when they change their behavior.

More than anything, what your kids need is to feel heard and understood. Your empathy is authentic; your ex's is an act. Let yours show. Your kids will feel it.

### Handling When Your Ex Undermines Your Authority

So what can you do? Let's say you're planning to take your child out to dinner, and they say, "I need to check with (your ex) to make sure it's OK." You can remind your child that you and your ex can each make the rules on your own parenting time. But that may not work.

According to AJ Gajjar, you might want to tell your child that if it helps them to feel better, then by all means, go ahead and call the other parent. In doing so, you're putting the power back into your child's hands. She says it's important, even amid these intense situations, to find opportunities to give our children agency; something they probably don't have with your ex. This can actually be an opportunity for them to learn problem-solving skills and build their decision-making muscles. Initially, the "check-with-my-other-parent" dynamic might come up repeatedly, but over time, giving kids a choice consistently helps them to feel safe.

The time will likely come when your child realizes that they really don't need to ask their other parent; they're just fine with you in your house with your rules. The key is letting them figure it out for themselves.

## Fostering Dependence in a Child

Our job as parents is to help our children not need us anymore, no matter how bittersweet that might be. We want kids to be able to function in the world without us.

Your toxic ex likely doesn't share that goal. They rely on your children to be their allies, and sometimes they might even treat your kids as peers or friends. Your ex may lead your child to feel unable to make any decision independently, or that something bad will happen if they try to do anything without their oversight.

Lisa, in her previous life, had a family member who never let her son have a voice. When he was really little and other people would ask him a question, his mother would jump in and answer for him. As he grew older and into adolescence, he just stopped talking. Even during dinners with family, he would be on his phone the entire time or sit looking down at the table.

You encourage your kids to spread their wings in healthy ways. Your ex creates a counter-narrative based on fear, and conditions your children to believe that they are "not ready" to be independent. Denied the opportunity to have choices, your child never develops a voice.

**Enmeshment**

Your child might come to feel like your ex's happiness is their responsibility, and that shouldering their emotional burdens is part of the job description. Enmeshment is sometimes described as *emotional incest*. It's when a child becomes like a therapist to a parent, or takes on the role of a trusted friend, or even a spouse.

When a toxic parent reverses the parent-child roles, that's *parentification*, and it's terribly unhealthy for children. It's a part of the early life experience that contributes to toxic family dynamics being perpetuated across generations.

Kids who are enmeshed with a parent are not allowed to separate or be their own person with independent self-esteem. The technical term for this process is *individuation,* and it's critical developmentally. If your child is unable to individuate, they may eventually seek the same power dynamics in their own future relationships that they witnessed in yours, making them perfect prey for an abuser of their own.

It's really important to make sure to give even very young kids age-appropriate choices. For example, you can let them know that they can have one of two vegetables laid out for dinner, or ask them which pair of pants or shoes they want to wear—and that it's up to them entirely. They learn that when they're with you, they get to choose. They see that with you, they have options, and that their opinions matter, even in the smallest way.

## You'll Need Courage

We've had more than one client who had internalized a false narrative from their ex that the children didn't want to hear from them, and that their continued attempts to repair broken relationships were actually causing more harm. This was far from the truth. Out of desperation, these targeted parents had again become susceptible to the manipulation of their exes and accepted advice from their alienating co-parent that was actually a part of their evil campaign to create pathological alignment between themselves and a child.

You're going to have to learn to be brave in ways you might not have ever considered before. According to author Kelly Corrigan, bravery requires a setting aside of self so that you are available for another person—in this case, your child—to lean on. Love sometimes is the opposite of action. In families, Corrigan says that bravery can be mostly "just sitting there." Remember how people generally love to talk…so let your kids have a voice!

## Questions for Reflection

How has your co-parent displayed these behaviors?

1. Encourage your child to believe you're mentally unfit, unpredictable, and possibly dangerous.
2. Make your child discard or replace things you've given them, including school supplies, clothing, and holiday gifts. This may also extend to presents from your extended family.
3. Make your child feel guilty for demonstrating any affection toward you or anyone associated with you.
4. Reject, shame, or punish your child emotionally for expressing positive feelings towards you.

5. Make insulting comments about you in front of or directly to your child.
6. Share inappropriate details with your child about your separation or the legal process.
7. Fail to follow the access schedule for parenting time.
8. Violate legal decision-making or other aspects of your parenting orders.
9. Minimize your presence, role, or importance in your child's life.

## CHAPTER 6

# OH. MY. GOD. (WHAT CAN I DO?)

*"We've been divorced for six years, and my ex has violated every other line of the parenting agreement!"*

—Been There Got Out client

### You are Not Powerless

One of our core values at Been There Got Out is to provide practical, actionable advice. If you're dealing with alienation, the foundation is understanding what it is, the damage it does, and how and why your ex would do something so reprehensible. We've done that. The rest of this book focuses on what you can do about it, and you are completely forgiven if you jumped straight to this chapter.

Although everything about parental alienation is bad, the good news is that there is a lot you can do to protect or restore your relationship with your children, and you have a few paths by which you can try to change things, including:

- Legal action
- Interactions with your children, even with little regular contact
- Your direct communication with your ex

So, please take a breath. As harrowing as this is, your kids—and your relationship with them—can be OK. It sometimes takes a Herculean effort, but your children are worth it.

### Signs You Need to Nip it in the Bud

When bad behavior occurs without any accountability, things can get much worse. As with most things, acting as quickly as you can is important, ideally, as soon as you realize that alienation is occurring. It's a lot easier to prevent a spill than to clean one up, so to speak. But what are the signals that should tell you that this *is* serious and it's time to do something?

According to psychiatry professor Dr. Richard A. Warshak, your case should be treated with the urgency given to cases with missing children because, for you, your children are essentially missing. The number one sign you need to watch for is when your ex stops following the parenting plan or visitation schedule. And the worst mistake you can make, according to attorney Ashish Joshi and several of our other attorney colleagues, is not immediately addressing this with the court.

When this kind of behavior goes on for a while, not only does your ex become emboldened, but it can seem like it didn't matter much because you allowed it to happen for so long. According to Joshi, judges often become frustrated when months or years have already passed and court-ordered parenting time has not been scrupulously followed. They may wonder, *Why is this the first time I'm hearing about this? Why wasn't the court involved sooner?* The more quickly you get it on the record, the better off you are, no matter how unappealing a return to the legal system might be.

Another red flag is when a child starts backing away from you. This can signify that there is something suspicious going on, and the key to fixing it is intervening as early as possible to reduce the risk of a child going further down the slope to the point of total rejection.

One of our clients agreed on a temporary parenting plan for their three children. From the get-go, his ex refused to follow it. Months passed, and things went from bad to worse in terms of his relationship with the kids. There had been no significant legal follow-up. His lawyer had put off getting an evaluator assigned. By the time the kids started therapy, it turned out the counselor was completely unskilled in domestic violence, and made matters worse by saying that the kids, including a nine-year-old, "had gotten used to it." She even suggested that the children themselves should decide what they wanted to do, and thus the status quo became the new normal.

Although it was much harder playing catch-up, a lot changed when he took things into his own hands and made sure their final agreement included consequences for his ex's failure to follow the parenting plan.

New Jersey psychologist and custody evaluator Dr. Mark Singer suggests therapeutic as well as legal interventions to make sure that a parent engaging in alienating behavior is made aware of what they're doing—because sometimes people don't even realize it—to give them an opportunity to change the behavior. He reiterates that children are best served by having healthy relationships with healthy parents, and if a child's relationship with one parent is being negatively impacted, it goes against what's best for a child.

## What Will it Take?

The only time your ex is going to stop is if they are called out for what they're doing, and we do not at all mean announcing to them that they're engaging in parental alienation. There are three battles that you may have to fight, which impact each other, and the actions you take in one area can support—or harm—the others:

1. The most critical: **counter the impact of their alienation on your children.** You need to do this whether or not you're able to change your ex's behavior.
2. Consider if and how you can take steps to **mitigate their alienating behavior in the first place.** This is really about reducing, containing, or cutting off the avenues they use, as it's unlikely you'll be able to shut it down entirely.
3. And craziest of all, you're probably going to have to **defend yourself against their claims that you're the one engaging in alienation** yourself. Remember all their lies in court? Those will surely continue, and you need to do all you can to ensure that they get zero traction in the legal system or anywhere else.

### Protecting Your Time

One of the most common ways your ex may try to steal your child's loyalty is by making it inconvenient for them to spend time with you, so they start to feel like your visits disrupt their routine. At some point, it is not just your ex who acts like you are an intrusion, but your child as well, who may come to believe that they have only one home and life, and it's not with you.

According to attorney Charles Jamieson, when you don't firmly assert your parenting rights, you could put yourself at a disadvantage in court by signaling that you don't care all that much. If your narrative includes domestic violence, but you left your kid with their other parent, it can appear as if you abandoned your child to the care of an abuser.

Before we met, one of our clients fled an abusive relationship with their children based on poor legal advice. She was forced to bring the kids back, but was so fearful of her ex that she left them with him full-time while seeking a geographical relocation. Back in court, the judge admonished her, questioning why, if her ex were so bad, she would have left two toddlers in his care. The relocation was a non-starter, and she struggled just to get back close to 50/50 parenting time, even after she moved back to the area.

## What About a Cooling Off Period?

Even in intact families, it's customary to deal with drama, especially when there are teens in the picture; challenges are part of normal growth and development. In families with extreme dynamics, sometimes a small argument can quickly turn into a deep rift where your child doesn't want to see you…indefinitely.

We see lawyers and other professionals mistakenly suggest that you "step back" to let the child have a cooling off period, and not to do anything legally because "it might make matters worse." Letting your child stay with your ex on your time could be fine if you're talking about a day or two. But if it continues to happen and your relationship with your child is getting worse, it may be necessary to take swift action.

Remember, it can take a while for anything to happen in the legal system, starting with the amount of time it takes just to get a court date. A judge is generally not able to order specific mental health or legal intervention without first having some kind of evidentiary hearing. For that, witnesses, including evaluators and therapists, are required, and it takes time for everyone to prepare. This is why it is so important to seek intervention immediately and not wait until things get out of hand.

## Breathing Room?

Having children pull away or refuse contact is heartbreaking. Stepping back to "give the kids space," and not continuing to try to have contact often does not go well outside of court, either, especially as a child tries to make sense of why you've pulled back.

Another of our clients had a tween son who had been physically attacking her in the first couple of years after the divorce. His father had promised to take him every other week, but got into a new relationship and disappeared for more than a year. Their son's aggressive behavior toward his mother was clearly stemming from the boy's sense of abandonment.

A couple of years later, her ex remarried and moved back into town. Although she had primary physical and legal custody, he managed to interfere with their relationship, including badmouthing her to all the parents on their son's baseball team. She withdrew for a while, feeling like everyone had turned against her. When she finally built up the courage to again come to one of her son's games, he screamed that he "hated" her in front of all his teammates because she had "abandoned" him.

Looking back, she can see now why staying away out of fear had only helped solidify the poisonous messages her ex had sent to their son: she didn't care enough about him to be in his life.

## Urgent Action

We know that in courtrooms throughout the world, people believe that parents have a right to be in their children's lives, barring evidence of abuse or neglect. But your ex may make you feel stripped of this right, claiming that the kids don't want to see you anyway. It can feel so hopeless.

On initial calls with people early in the divorce process, one of the most common things we hear is a fear that their ex will make derogatory comments behind their backs to their children, about what a terrible person they are. In our practice we are known for our "harsh New York reality check" when it comes to such matters, and as such, stress to our clients that it's important to plan on their exes saying terrible things about them. You can't do much to make it stop, but there are certainly steps you can take early on to protect yourself both personally and legally.

According to Ashish Joshi, going for detailed orders, ensuring parent-child contact is step one. Penalties for violations of these orders should be included, and when this occurs, moving quickly for sanctions is step two. The worst thing that can happen is, unfortunately, something we see pretty frequently, and that's when your ex repeatedly violates the orders, nothing is done, and this becomes the new standard.

## Instinctive (and Uneducated) Responses

Whether or not you know what you're experiencing has a name and is part of an intentional campaign by your ex, most parents realize that something is wrong, and react understandably: staking out the moral high ground for yourself by making triple-certain that you're not doing anything wrong.

You make sure you're doing all you can to shield the children from the slightest conflict between you and your ex. If you're still in face-to-face contact, you keep anything controversial out of earshot when the kids are around. And you never, ever badmouth them in front of your children, as you already know how tough the breakup of the family unit is.

After all, two wrongs don't make a right ... right? You probably learned during the divorce process how important it is to have "clean hands" yourself, since although your ex could mess up a hundred ways, your first minor slip could spin the narrative into looking like you are the problem. "I would never do that; I don't say anything bad about my ex!" Our communication is 93% non-verbal, which emanates from our facial expressions, tone of voice, and energy. Our children are watching all of these cues, especially when we roll our eyes, sigh, or avoid conversations.

After her own separation, UK founder of the Single Mama Club, Katie Ripman, attended a co-parenting communication class, which exposed a number of unconscious behaviors she herself was doing, which she realized many other parents do without realizing the impact on their children. Katie learned that her first mistake occurred during exchanges (or *handovers*, as they say in the UK). Although she was acting positive, upbeat, and welcoming to her children, and even giving her ex a quick hello, she was not making eye contact, which was significantly affecting her daughters.

All of our clients are victims of domestic violence, not just mental, emotional, or physical violence, and we know it can be terrifying to look your ex in the face. It's certainly something that takes preparation and practice, but if and when you do it, you're also modeling to your children that you are not afraid. Katie started experimenting during exchanges to consciously look at her ex, and noticed a palpable change in her daughters' comfort level.

### Who Are You and What Did You Do with My Mom?

We all feel more comfortable when we know what's next. Katie told her girls ahead of time that she was going to "have a quick chat with Daddy today, because I never talk to him and I feel like it would just be better for us as a family if I start talking to him just a little bit more."

We need to acknowledge that a child might be jarred by your suddenly acting completely different. Katie says that letting the kids know ahead of time is a way to give them a heads up so they don't think that you're acting fake.

Eye contact and small talk are a big deal in our community, and we imagine neither will be easy. This is going to take time, so Katie suggests that you "habit stack" by first looking at what it is that you want to change and take it one step at a time.

### Are You Unloading in Front of Your Kids?

*"Aren't you divorced yet! Are you STILL in court!"* We often catch up with friends at kids' events like birthday parties, and they want to know what's going on. But it's not a good idea to have these conversations when the kids are nearby or under the same roof, not necessarily because they can hear you, but because they will know what you're saying and who you're talking about from your body language, tone, and your face. Even if you're all the way at the other end of the room, they are watching. So save it for when you have complete privacy to unload.

Derogatory nicknames for our exes are a popular topic that we have shared many laughs over. However, when Lisa was putting together exhibits for her case years ago, a lawyer told her she could not submit anything "with *that* name at the top." It's off-brand for us to share what it was, but oops!

You never want to have to submit discovery of this nature to your ex's attorney, either; we want to make sure that they don't have any ammunition to use against you.

And it's not just a judge you need to worry about. Kids love snooping and are great at getting into our phones. If your child sees you use an insulting name for their other parent, they inadvertently become privy to a poisonous message you are putting out into the world.

## Questions for Reflection

1. Of the three main "problems to solve" we discussed in Chapter 1 (getting the best co-parenting arrangement, insulating yourself against false claims, and protecting your relationship with your children), which feels most urgent in your situation right now, and why?
2. What violations of your parenting plan or concerning behaviors have you been "letting slide" that you now realize need immediate attention?

## CHAPTER 7

# GETTING YOURSELF RIGHT

*"If your kids are going to be okay, they need their parents to be okay."*

—Most experts

In major wars involving territorial conquest, military commanders know the importance of winning the hearts and minds of the populace. It's far easier to take and hold land when the people who live there are on your side. When they're not, you need to invest more resources in preventing uprisings that could destabilize your efforts and harm your overall campaign.

The same is true in this fight. You want as many people—whether they're directly involved or not—on your side. The last thing you need is a teacher expressing concerns about how you parent, or a doctor siding with the views of your ex. Dealing with alienation requires a strategic, holistic approach (another of our core values). Like many of life's big challenges, it starts with getting yourself right. We'll get into your parenting with your kids in Chapters 12, 13, and 14; this is about how you conduct yourself and how to properly gear up for the battle you may have already been in for a while. Bear in mind that this is a tough road; you need to be sure you're up to it.

**Your Behavior**

Most parents don't go to Little League games to meet their new best friend. They show up to root on and support their kid and the team, and share a wonderful part of their childhood.

Chris' ex is the big, showy, flamboyant type who tries to be the life of the party. During their three-year divorce and subsequent co-parenting years, she went to great lengths to do all she could to establish social ties with other adults in the ecosystem of their boys' lives. She volunteered for class field trips and would attend every event tied to their children's activities, regardless of whose parenting time it was, sitting right up front at any performance, cheering the loudest, and making a spectacle of herself while doing everything she could to make Chris feel unwelcome. And it did make Chris, who wasn't yet far enough along in his recovery, uncomfortable, as he didn't yet see that the community wasn't buying into the performance.

We hear the line, "My ex has everyone fooled," a lot from our people. And it's just not true; a lot of people don't fall for their schtick. Narcissists and other toxic personalities turn a lot of people off. Although it may appear that everyone is cozying up to your ex, most people keep them at arm's length. If they're aware of the conflict between the two of you, they don't want to get involved. They just act the part because it's the easiest and most sociably acceptable way to behave.

Think for a moment about your ex's life history. How many healthy, close, long-term relationships do they really have? Do they have deep friendships that have lasted many years? Upon close, honest inspection, the answer is probably "no."

You probably already have a sense for how few people understand personality disorders and high-conflict divorce (including those in the divorce profession), and are not likely to find a sympathetic audience in the social circles that sprout up around your children. The other parents just want to live their lives, support their kids, and enjoy whatever the activity is. So try to be nice, get along, and don't talk about how awful your ex is, because nobody wants to hear it.

Our client, who began attending her son's baseball games again, had stayed away more by a sense of being exiled from the group of parents than by fear of her ex. She was terrified that they all believed whatever horrible things he'd said about her. To her surprise, when she showed up alone and sat in the back row of the bleachers, hiding her face, four families surrounding her turned around and asked where and how she'd been. One woman even followed up with an invitation for drinks, saying that they had missed her.

It can be so hard while still getting your feet under you, but please try to understand that the social groups that form and disband repeatedly during your kids' childhoods are not likely to be a permanent peer group that you'll share with your ex. These people probably don't care about the conflict between the two of you, and even if they do, they don't matter. More importantly, they are not likely to have any influence on custody or your relationship with your kids over the long term.

## With Teachers, Doctors, Therapists, and Other Professionals

Unlike social groups, the professionals who work with your children and both of you do matter—or they might—when it comes to both legal proceedings and your child's welfare. So you should care what these people think of you, but the rest of what we just said applies with the professionals, too: they don't want to be involved with the drama, and they don't care about anything other than doing their job and getting on with their day.

But the same emotional paranoia applies: Does this teacher hate me because of my ex's smear campaign? Does the therapist believe that I'm the problem? Sometimes, there can be at least a little validity to these fears. Your ex is probably going to try the same tactics that they use in your social circles with professionals in an attempt to poison your relationships with them or even draw them into your custody battle.

This is not the time to fight fire with fire. Always remember that good professionals are *conflict-averse*. They're just trying to do a job, and anything that even feels like a lawsuit waiting to happen will, in all likelihood, repel them.

Melissa Lowry, Headmistress of Christ the King School in Atlanta, says that a school's job is to be neutral and supportive of both parents. Legally, they are not allowed to take sides. The school is obligated to follow parenting plans, not weigh in on them. Still, your ex, overtly or subtly, is probably going to try to win them over. They're always looking to weaponize anyone they can in their all-out campaign to destroy you. So what do you do?

Chris had a lot of success with two different variations of a script suggested to him by someone years ago that he would love to thank and credit here, but he just does not remember who. Whoever you were, please know that we've done a lot to develop the basic idea over the years, and you have our—and many of our clients'—gratitude for sharing it with us. We call this the *Unemotional Preemptive Strike* or *UPS* framework, and it can be super useful.

## The *UPS* Framework

The basic template goes like this (using Joe as the child's name):

> *Unfortunately, Joe's mom and I do not have a good relationship. All I ask is, if she should ever say anything about me that raises any concerns, that you please give me the opportunity to respond before forming an opinion.*

This *UPS* script is very carefully worded, so let's break it down. **First**, the word "unfortunately" says a lot. You find the situation regrettable. You wish it weren't so. You have tried, but you haven't been able to fix it. It's not you, it's your ex.

**Second,** saying that you don't have a good relationship states the fact simply and without any emotion. It's almost underwhelmingly worded when you consider how important it is for co-parents to try to get along. The matter-of-fact verbiage implies that the situation has existed for a while, and you have moved past the emotion that was likely involved. It displays maturity.

**Third**, you're making a very reasonable request. You're not asking them to side with you. You're appealing to a sense of fairness, which most people have. We're not pressuring anybody to believe us; we're just asking for the opportunity to give our side of the story. And it's not an opportunity. "An" opportunity is something they need to make for you. "The" opportunity is something that is already there, and rightfully yours. And how would they feel if they didn't give you that opportunity, went ahead and formed an opinion without hearing both sides? That wouldn't be very professional, would it? That could lead to making a mistake that affects the quality of their work and professional reputation.

**Fourth**, you're preparing the person for conflict coming from your ex. Remember: they are probably conflict-averse. You're giving them a warning of what might be on the horizon so that they won't be blindsided. And since you're giving them a heads-up, it's better if *you* can have this conversation first, so when your ex does say whatever they say, the professional is already prepared. But don't worry if you don't get to deliver your line first. It will still accomplish everything you need.

Parent-teacher conferences can be emotional torture or, in extreme cases, dangerous to do together with a toxic ex. As soon as possible after learning who his kids would have for a teacher in the new school year, Chris would say:

"I'm so sorry, but Joe's mom and I unfortunately do not have a good relationship. It's not safe, and it's certainly not healthy, for us to be in the same physical space. I know this is inconvenient, but would it be possible for us to have separate parent/teacher meetings?"

We won't break this one down in all the detail that we did with the first, but note the tone this sets. You're being very reasonable and asking for something that is admittedly an "inconvenience," but how much trouble is that in comparison to a situation that is potentially *unsafe*? The overall idea of the UPS Framework is to come across as innocent. You want to appear above the fray and show the emotional maturity of acceptance—*hey, I wish this were different, but there's nothing I can do about it, so I'm just going to carry on and do the best I can to be a great parent.*

You can do a lot with this framework!

## Common Mistakes to Avoid

People in our community who are dealing with the effects of alienation can experience such overwhelming frustration that they feel compelled to take action. Bear in mind that acting on impulses can sometimes be misguided, and worse, sabotage your legal case or exacerbate, rather than ease, the impact of the alienation. We strongly suggest you avoid the temptation to do any of the following:

1) **The Temptation of Social Media**

> "Social media is my therapy. I need people to hear my story. Besides, it doesn't affect our kids, because they're never gonna see my posts."
>
> —DT, one of many people dealing with high-conflict co-parenting

For a person who has been the target of abuse, not being believed serves to compound the trauma and pain. Phrases like *Why didn't you just leave?* or *Why doesn't the judge just ___?* can cut so deep, even if the motivation comes from a caring, innocent place.

One thing we see a lot in our coaching practice—and also experienced ourselves —is a feeling that *nobody understands what I'm going through.* These situations, not just alienation, but the broader experience of high-conflict relationships, divorce, custody battles, and co-parenting nightmares, are beyond anything most people can even comprehend. Those who haven't been through it themselves find the stories so crazy that their first reaction is disbelief, and this is true even of those closest to you and professionals who you'd think would understand.

Our clients are frequently the victims of smear campaigns and feel like they have been cast out of an entire community, so it's completely natural to want to share the other side of the story to disprove the lies. Motivated by a desire for someone—anyone—to understand, some people take to social media as a platform to do exactly that.

Don't! Here's why…first, you can be sure that your ex and their attorney are scouring your posts for anything they can twist and use against you. Even if you're telling the complete truth, saying negative things about your ex could support their claims that you're so angry that you're incapable of co-parenting cooperatively. It's also an easy leap for a judge to make, from seeing you bash your ex in a social media post to imagining you sending the same message, consciously or unconsciously, to your children.

Many separation agreements include something called a *non-disparagement clause*, which commits you to not talking negatively about your co-parent in front of your children or publicly. You do not want the other side to gain any traction at all with an argument that you are in violation.

A number of our clients, before meeting us, made the mistake of using social media as therapy and posted inappropriate details, which resulted in fines, sanctions, and even prohibition from posting anything ever, as ordered by the judge.

Canadian attorney Sean Valentine says that if you start blasting your ex on social media, you may be hit with a cease and desist order. If you ignore that, you could be putting yourself at risk of being held in contempt, which could have a variety of repercussions, including limiting your ability to defend yourself.

Difficult as it can be to muzzle yourself, the simplest and most foolproof solution is to just not say anything at all about your ex or your case on social media, or anywhere that could leave a digital footprint. Journaling is an excellent alternative.

**2) Withhold money that's owed.** Sometimes, a parent becomes so angry at the injustice they are experiencing that they refuse to make a mandated child support or alimony payment. Regardless of how you feel, follow court orders and keep your side of the street clean. You cannot give the opposition fodder to distract from the most important issue you are in court over.

3) **Write letters of frustration.** It's understandable if you're furious, but you should not be venting to the court. Instead, write "letters never to be sent." It's important to get out your feelings; just do it privately, not to court professionals who have influence in your case.

4) **Explain your ex's bad behavior to your children.** It is very tempting to convey to your kids that they are being brainwashed. This usually gets nowhere and would be viewed negatively by a judge. Lisa's ex sent several emails to their children bashing her during their years in court, which created a very poor impression for every judge involved with her case. You cannot show your child how angry you are toward your ex. According to a New York child therapist, Dr. Jill Leibowitz, if you cannot get yourself under control, then your child will not feel safe with you, either.

5) **Involve your children in court matters.** You don't want to share what's happening regarding your court case with your children. Unless you have absolutely no choice, keep the kids out of it.

6) **Refuse to go to supervised visitation.** It can feel deeply humiliating for someone who has always been a good parent to suddenly need some kind of chaperone just to spend time with their kids. Even if you know that you've done nothing wrong, not showing up to supervised visitation sends the message that your own ego is more important than spending time with your child. It can also be a missed opportunity, as professional supervisors will sometimes write reports that can support your legal case. Make sure that you use whatever opportunity you can to keep in contact with your kids.

7) **Cut off your ex's access to information.** Revoking your ex's security clearance for things like your child's patient portal with

the pediatrician, school accounts, health insurance accounts, or scheduling information in response to what they're doing is likely to be viewed as petty, vindictive, and uncooperative. Your ex and their attorney could paint a picture of you being the problem.

**8) Retaliate in other ways in violation of your agreement.** Your parenting plan is your own personal constitution, a binding legal document that governs your co-parenting life. Even if there doesn't appear to be any chance that you'll end up back in court, we always want our people to have clean hands, which in this case means sticking to your legal orders. If you violate the agreement even a fraction of the times that your ex does, that can give the other side ammunition to support a narrative that it's not them; it's both of you.

## Check Yourself Before You Wreck Yourself

Here are a few ways, inspired by conflict resolution expert Bill Eddy and others, to ensure you are doing the best you can outside of court, under trying circumstances:

1. **Remember the good stuff.** Make sure to note any positive qualities about the other parent to your child. We often do an exercise with our clients before they meet with an evaluator, asking them to describe a couple of wonderful qualities about *their ex*. Although most of them find this a repulsive exercise, it's helpful for presentation and should also be used with your children. We want you to try hard to remember the positive qualities that drew you to your ex, even if you hate them; imagine what you can still value for your kids. Remember, your child is half your ex, so you are enhancing their self-identity by validating their other parent.

One example Lisa uses is to note how her ex was very smart, and she loved how much he enjoyed reading. He used to read to their son every night before he went to sleep, and their son grew up loving books. Lisa always acknowledged her ex's influence and how it shaped their son in a positive way.

2. **Apologize for the negative.** Everyone slips up and says bad things about their ex during and post-separation. That's normal, but if you have badmouthed your ex to your kids, make sure you use a *repairing* comment. First, apologize verbally to your child for making a disparaging remark about your ex, and then note something positive. If you can, acknowledge that you were just upset and that it is not their responsibility to emotionally support you.

This can be extraordinarily difficult, but your kids need to see at least one parent show accountability for their own behavior, so it's going to have to be you! Doing this also models that we all make mistakes at times, and can learn to say, *I'm sorry.*

3. **Don't only support the negative.** Humans say all kinds of things about each other. Kids will watch your reaction, so make sure you are not giving all your attention only to the negative statements they make about their other parent.

If the comments are concerning, make sure to get another professional involved so that it's not just you making statements about your ex's abuse, especially while legal proceedings are going on. CPS investigators have told us that, when they get a report from one parent during a custody battle, they are less likely to take it seriously because of the timing and the source. You always need evidence to back up your claims, and your testimony is generally not the strongest when it comes to reporting your ex's abuse of your child. Make sure you have other eyes on it.

4. **Teach your children how to advocate for themselves.** There are plenty of toxic people in this world, and your child is going to have to learn how to deal with them. Children with a difficult parent, unfortunately and fortunately, acquire crucial social and emotional skills, particularly regarding boundaries, because they have to learn how to stand up for themselves with their own parent.

Mental health coach Susie Pettit noticed that her kids, now young adults, learned valuable negotiation skills that she never developed in her youth. As a parent, she learned to *step out of the God role* and have faith that she had done everything she could for them, trusting that perhaps they were having these hardships for the sake of becoming the most amazing people.

5. **Keep your intimacy in check.** We may not realize how much we depend on our children to meet our own emotional needs. What you're going through is isolating, but your child should not be looked at as the solution to this problem.

Eddy advises that to avoid your child's unhealthy dependency on you, it might be better not to have them sleep regularly with you in your bed except during infancy.

Likewise, don't confide in your child about adult decisions and information.

New York City therapist Dr Jill Liebowitz says that kids dealing with divorce are "perpetually experiencing loss" because when they are with one parent, it means they are separated from the other. Don't add to this by announcing how much you miss them when they are at your ex's home. With young children, she recommends that you say before transitions, "I know you're going to miss me when we're not together, and I'll miss you, but I know you're going to have a good time with Mommy/Daddy when you're with them."

For young children, she thinks having some kind of transitional object, like a bracelet, which is a tie or connection to you, can be helpful. When your child is away, it can be an opportunity to start putting yourself together again and finding things you enjoy doing. When they return, share what you did so they know you're just fine without them.

One of our clients told us that when her son left, she would literally lie on the floor and cry for hours. During our conversation, she realized her mother had done the same thing, and she'd always felt responsible and worried when she'd go to her dad's. After that talk, she began making a concerted effort to go to movies with friends and started mountain biking again. Her life has completely turned around for the better, and her son is thriving.

6. **Watch it with comparisons.** Your child views themself as being made up of both of you. Don't compare your talents, skills, and characteristics with those of your ex's, and certainly don't emphasize your ex's flaws to your child.

7. **Get support.** If you haven't realized by now, we are all about a team effort in getting you through this. The best thing you can do for your child is to get as emotionally healthy as possible. Model taking care of yourself, so that

your children do not feel that they are wholly responsible for taking care of others.

8. **Model bravery.** With support, you are going to learn courage in ways you might never have imagined.

   Being brave does not mean taking over and becoming the hero. We know well the instinct to try to fix and manage things. When we swoop in like this, author Kelly Corrigan says, we make ourselves the center of attention, which is a space reserved for your child. Because then, rather than being the helper, we become one of the afflicted.

   To be brave is to be available and to understand that, even if you can't help, you can keep loving, supportive space reserved for your child. And sometimes that's the toughest, best thing you can do.

## Questions for Reflection

1. Consider public settings like your child's school events or activities. Are you avoiding these situations out of fear, or showing up but letting your ex's presence intimidate you?

2. Using the *UPS* framework, practice introducing yourself to a new professional in your child's life. How would you present the situation with your ex in a way that sounds mature and reasonable while preparing them for what you imagine your ex will throw their way? Write out your specific script and practice it.

3. Looking at the eight guidelines for checking yourself (remembering good qualities about your ex, apologizing for mistakes, not supporting only negative comments, etc.), which area do you most need to work on?

## CHAPTER 8

# GEARING UP FOR A(NOTHER) LEGAL BATTLE

*"Get as much proof as possible...proof is king."*

—Leona Krasner, Attorney

### Resolution?

California attorney Brian Pakpour has told us that alienating behaviors are a problem that the family court has to figure out how to address. Even when there's proof, remedies are limited. Judges don't often have the appropriate answers, which is why it's so important for you to bring potential solutions to the table.

Pakpour once had a difficult case with a two-week trial that included a number of expert witnesses. His client successfully showed that her ex had been alienating their son, and she was awarded 100% custody in terms of time. However, it ended up being a nightmare. The child was a teenager at the time, and even after some therapy sessions, Pakpour's client ended up agreeing to go back to 50/50 because her son had been so deeply affected that he was verbally abusive with his mother and her partner, who was also part of the case.

Pakpour believes that all the time, money, and energy spent on getting this big "win" wasn't worth it because the damage had unfortunately already been done. Proof doesn't automatically lead to an easy resolution.

## The Five-Factor Model

Invisible abuse can be hard to prove. Because it's often difficult to figure out why a child refuses contact with a parent, by the time one of these claims makes it to family court, we need to come in with a lot more than labels.

In his book, *Litigating Parental Alienation*, Ashish Joshi uses Dr. Amy Baker's Five-Factor Model as a basis for providing effective documentation for alienation, which is through meticulous, careful preparation. The following are factors to consider when building a persuasive case:

1. **How is the child actively avoiding a visit, resisting, or refusing a relationship with you?** Are they crying at drop-offs? Not responding over a series of weeks or months to any of your attempts to text them?

2. **Was there a prior positive relationship between you and your child?** Do you have birthday cards they sent you, or anything that shows their former affection for you, such as photos of the two of you together?

3. **Was there abuse, neglect, or seriously deficient parenting on your part before being rejected?** Is there anything someone can point to that shows you harmed your child, directly or indirectly?

4. **What are the various alienating behaviors that your ex has been using?** Has your ex sent poisonous messages about you, blocked communication, or refused to follow

the parenting plan? Think of this in the context of the in-depth descriptions and examples we shared in Chapters 4 and 5.

5. **Does the child exhibit any of the behavioral manifestations of alienation?** Is their rejection chronic and/or unjustified? Are you the only target of your child's rage?

## The Fork in the Road

The decision on how to prosecute your case is not a matter of whether alienation is happening; instead, it becomes how to approach your case legally to best achieve your goals. We imagine the outcome should be the opportunity to have a healthy relationship with your child. Which approach might get there more effectively: portraying your ex as a monster (which goes against the significant value of acknowledging the role of both parents in your child's life), or instead demonstrating the issues and their impact, proposing solutions to these problems? We believe the latter, with the bonus being that a judge or evaluator may view you as more child-focused.

How can we avoid labels while allowing others to draw their own conclusions? The difference is in the presentation.

## I Can't Get My Kid to Go

To be deprived of your right to parenting time, the law would have to require a finding that access to you would endanger your child physically or significantly impair their emotional development, says Ashish Joshi. Without this finding, parenting time has to be respected and enforced.

If your ex argues that they can't make your kid comply with court-ordered parenting time, your lawyer should remind the court that allowing a child to believe following court orders is optional for them amounts to *psychological maltreatment*, which is "verbal or symbolic acts given by a parent or caregiver which can result in significant psychological harm." When your ex claims that they are "encouraging" your child to go visit you, they are allowing your child to choose, which puts them in the middle by inviting them to pick sides.

If you already have a stipulated parenting plan, your ex is making a huge legal blunder by admitting that they are not complying with that court order. Dr. Amy Baker suggests asking your ex to define what "encouraging" means, as the choice is not your child's to make.

Baker asks us to imagine what would happen if our child needed life-saving surgery and they didn't want it. If they wanted to do drugs, drop out of school, or join a gang? We bet you would find a way to compel the child to do what was right.

> "We don't encourage people to wear seatbelts. We don't encourage children to go to school. We don't encourage them to take their vitamins. We make them. We create an environment where the child knows we're not going to drive until they've buckled their seatbelt, and they want it buckled because they understand that it protects them."
>
> —Dr. Amy Baker

The best way to shut this down with your child is to say that the schedule was made by both parents, and you're both obligated to follow it, no questions asked.

### You're Either a Liar or an Ineffective Parent

One of our clients had a teenager who didn't want to go visit her father. When she argued in court that her daughter, seventeen at the time, had her own car and could just drive away on her own, the judge rebuked her, asking, "Who's in charge at your house?" Dr. Baker says that a parent who is not making their child comply with a court-ordered schedule "cannot have it both ways." How can you be a competent, effective parent but magically be unable to make your child do something they have to do? The one caveat is if there's a finding of abuse, it's a whole other story. If one of our clients decides not to comply with a court-ordered schedule, we stress how important it is that they have compelling evidence as a strong defense.

## An Ounce of Prevention in Parenting Plans

Given that you are likely dealing with an ex who will attempt to undermine your relationship during your access time, your best protection from the very beginning is to make sure you have an airtight parenting plan that allows for minimal interruption to parenting time, depending on the schedule. It's unfortunate to have to acknowledge that these cases cannot be treated as "normal" co-parenting, where each parent supports and encourages your child's relationship with the other, but in situations like these, building guardrails into the parenting plan can make a huge difference.

## How Do I Prove Parental Alienation?

New York City divorce lawyer Yoni Levoritz says that since "parental alienation is not an actual psychiatric or psychological diagnosis," there are no firm legal statutes for it. Litigating an alienation case, whether you're accusing or defending against a false claim by the other side, is inherently complex. You may benefit from a mechanism that judges can lean on when they need to dig a bit deeper.

In most jurisdictions, the family court can call in a third party to represent the interests of children in contentious custody situations. This person may be called a guardian ad litem (GAL), minor's counsel, an attorney for the child (AFC), or something else. Their specific role and authority can vary as much as the labels. (For our purposes in this book, we'll use these titles interchangeably.) Broadly speaking, all such professionals are there to get to know your case and your child more intimately than a judge can. Sometimes, judges will proactively order that a GAL be appointed. Or you may want to ask the court to do this yourself. These professionals can help with a variety of situations, and good ones can be worth their weight in gold (keep in mind that they're not all good!)

When a parent involves children in court matters, it can contribute to their anxiety, and most judges understand this. New York City AFC Stephanie (she does not share her last name publicly) has noted that, in working with her clients, all of whom are children, she has seen situations where a parent would not stop discussing the case with the child, causing them guilt, discomfort, and fear. Stephanie had to report to the court that if that parent kept pushing to where it was affecting the child's ability to express themself honestly, she would have to take a position based on her own opinion.

If your AFC/GAL raises this issue with the judge, and your ex continues to involve your child in court matters, Levoritz says that your ex could be exposed to contempt, economic sanctions, and potentially supervised visitation. Remember, a GAL's job is to help your child have a voice. You can explain to the GAL how your child is being continuously dragged into the litigation process and ask for an order to prevent it. It can be difficult to prove that your ex is engaging in alienating behaviors, but this is an instance where recording conversations with your child can help paint a picture, according to Levoritz.

We do not recommend bringing recordings like this to a judge. Custody evaluator Dr. Mark Singer says that cases where people have audio and video recordings can be problematic because you don't have the full context of what happened. If you can identify and document specific behaviors, Singer has found that sometimes the other parent will admit to them because they are unaware of what harm is being caused and that they are incriminating themselves. For example, he had a father acknowledge that they told their child that his mother was "mentally ill" because years beforehand, she had been diagnosed with depression. Regardless of how true such a statement might be, there is no reason your child would need to know something like this.

## My Ex Sabotages

Many people experiencing alienation think it's not that bad until they suddenly realize that it indeed is, and has been for years. One way to figure out where things stand is to track what's happening in real time. Dr. Baker recommends keeping a journal and noting dates and comments that kids make. It can be surprising to see that these kinds of poisonous messages may be occurring a lot more than you imagined. The important thing is that you are conscious of your ex's efforts, and documenting the patterns can be an eye-opener. This information will also be very helpful later as you start putting a case together for your lawyer, an evaluator, or a judge. We describe the terrible things your ex does that are simultaneously difficult to deal with and helpful to your legal case, *usefully awful*.

When your ex is blocking contact, it's important that you do all you can to preserve whatever contact you do have, no matter what, even if it's just mailing letters. Sending cards to mark important dates is significant; even adult children notice when you do not send one on their birthday. It shows that you care, even if you don't talk anymore.

Attorney Charles Jamieson recommends that you also make copies of whatever you send, whether they are letters, cards, or gifts. Take photographs of any tangible proof you have that you have made the effort to stay involved with your child, as this kind of evidence can be very helpful in court.

## Collateral and Relevant Evidence

Compelling cases should be built around factors the court cares about, one of which is that parents should support each other's role in their child's life.

Ashish Joshi notes that evidence may reveal *triangulation* by an alienating parent to enlist professionals as their allies in a campaign to destroy your relationship with your child. For example, CPS reports may disclose that your ex provided specific details to the worker, knowing they were false. Doctors' records may also show a pattern of your ex using appointments to accuse you of inappropriate behavior. If this occurs in front of your child, as it often does, the damage is compounded.

One of our clients' exes brought their daughter to her pediatrician and announced that she was "ready to talk" about her father's sexual abuse against her sibling, not only fabricating an abuse claim, but also pressuring their daughter to become actively involved in their court case.

When these kinds of things occur in private sessions with professionals who are also mandated reporters, the goal of an alienating parent is often to get the professional to record the information so that it gets put into the child's permanent medical record. This might later be used as proof of your "inappropriate behavior," without anything to verify that it is true.

In states like New Jersey, which have strong coercive control laws, someone who does this can be subject to legal sanctions. You can show tangible proof of your relationship with your child through a variety of evidence types, including:

- Photographs
- Video and audio recordings
- Cards for birthdays and other occasions
- Emails
- Voicemails
- Letters
- Records
- Eyewitnesses

Dr. Mark Singer suggests that sometimes friends, relatives, teachers, and other people who know your child can provide information that can support or refute parental alienation allegations, but this is not enough.

If outside agencies have been involved with your case, get copies of:

- CPS reports
- Police reports
- Witness statements
- Child's medical records
- Child's mental health records

## Documentation: Where To Start

Joshi suggests that you make a list of all of the things you have been accused of, including the following details:

1. **How exactly have you been portrayed to your children by your ex?** Be specific. We like to think of those "three U's" from Chapter 4. How has your ex painted you as *unsafe, unloving,* or *unavailable* to your child?
2. **Is this portrayal accurate in any way?** Was it ever? For example, if you were an active addict and your behavior impacted your parenting, be honest. Were you ever arrested or convicted of something related to a substance issue, such as a DUI? Did you lose your job? Were there any incidents that others were witness to?
3. **What happened with your child during this time?** Were they old enough to be aware that there was ever an issue? Were they rejecting you then, possibly out of fear? And was this prior to separation or divorce?
4. **Why is the portrayal inaccurate now? What has changed?** Here, start focusing on what you've done to address the problem. Have you been sober or in recovery? For how long? What kinds of support do you have now that you didn't have in the past, such as an accountability partner, successful completion of anger management classes, co-parenting courses, or anything that shows your growth or dedication to being a better parent and person?
5. **How do we prove that this portrayal is false?** Think about the evidence you have to show that what's been said about you is untrue. We will be talking about very specific pieces of tangible evidence you might want to gather to answer this particular question shortly. For example,

could you provide collateral witnesses who could testify to what's changed, if needed?

## Documenting Communication Between Your Ex and Your Child

Connecticut attorney Kevin L. Hoffkins says that if you feel that your ex may be disparaging you to your child, it's important to "monitor their communications." Take a look at texts or any kind of social media messaging that can be accessed to see if there are derogatory comments by your ex. This is great evidence to bring to court to show how they may be undermining your relationship. He says that you might be able to get an order that they can't communicate with the child through these channels.

Ashish Joshi suggests getting a court order to compel your ex and the children to produce electronic devices for forensic examination, such as smartphones, in which you might find a ton of relevant information that could expose their campaign to brainwash your child into rejecting you. Depending on the severity, this could also justify your asking for supervised visitation for your ex, as this kind of behavior is psychologically damaging to a child.

## The Children's Bill of Rights

We've talked a lot about using "best interests" factors, as well as alienation factors, but there's a whole other set of rights that you may use to demonstrate the harm your ex's behavior is causing your child. Many U.S. states and some countries have adopted a Children's Bill of Rights, which is typically more of a broad policy statement than an official part of family law. These documents describe basic protections that should be afforded to children when their parents separate, and are intended as a guide for parents and professionals to make sure a child's well-being is prioritized. We have had several clients cite these protections effectively in arguing their custody cases, and these Bills of Rights may give you a way to approach your case from yet another angle.

Google can help you find any similar document that may have been adopted in your own jurisdiction. Here's New York State's version of the Bill of Rights for Children Whose Parents Are Divorced or Separated (many others look similar):

1. The right not to be asked to "choose sides" between their parents.
2. The right not to be told the details of bitter or nasty legal proceedings going on between their parents.
3. The right not to be told "bad things" about the other parent's personality or character.
4. The right to privacy when talking to either parent on the telephone.
5. The right not to be cross-examined by one parent after spending time with the other parent.
6. The right not to be asked to be a messenger from one parent to the other.
7. The right not to be asked by one parent to tell the other parent untruths.
8. The right not to be used as a confidant regarding the legal proceedings between the parties.
9. The right to express feelings, whatever those feelings may be.
10. The right to choose not to express certain feelings.
11. The right to be protected from parental warfare.
12. The right not to be made to feel guilty for loving both parents.

New York attorney Leona Krasner notes that your documentation should revolve around each relevant factor, and the details of every violation that ties to it. Providing specificity when it comes to dates and summaries of events will strengthen your case if and when you need to go back to court. She compares this to a "Dear Diary situation on steroids."

## Documentation: Tying It Together

The best, most comprehensive organizational system we have found for cases like yours comes from something Ashish Joshi calls the "Clancy method." This trial planning and presentation methodology will keep your evidence and exhibits easy to access, and pave the way for you to save time, money, and energy as you gather together all necessary information. First, create a master document file, which includes a scan/PDF of every document, whether it's a transcript, statement, photograph, report, or anything else showing either your ex's alienating behavior or the visible impact of that behavior on the child.

Next, make a master chronology divided into three columns:

- **First column:** Include the **date** of each event of any significance.

- **Second column:** Lay out the **details** about each significant event: who, what, where, how, and why does this particular thing matter? Make sure to include a summary regarding your ex's behaviors and signs of alienation present in the child. Which of the alienation factors does it relate to?

- **Third column:** Here's where you make it easy for others to find the **exact location of the proof** needed for trial, meaning the page, paragraph, and/or line number of the relevant record to cross-reference with the master document file.

This detailed chronology will provide your evidentiary foundation for discovery, strategy, trial prep, and a roadmap to present evidence that supports your case. It's going to take time and focused effort, but having a comprehensive set of materials will impress any court professional you deal with and make it much easier for them to connect the dots and apply appropriate law.

Here is an example that includes several real-life examples we have heard throughout the years:

| Date/Factor | Description | Evidence |
| --- | --- | --- |
| 7/2/22<br><br>Poisonous messages | Father suddenly accused the long-term nanny (together for 9 years, and raised two of the children since birth) of inappropriately touching all three kids — boys and girls of various ages — during divorce proceedings. CPS investigated twice and dismissed. Children then said they didn't feel "safe" with Mom's choice of caregiver, that she had "poor judgment." The caregiver was so terrified and traumatized by the proceedings that she quit and went back to Barbados. Mom scrambled to find childcare; father destroyed familial attachment, and Mom's job was jeopardized. | Binder tab 5, p. 17-26 (includes CPS findings, text message chain) |

| | | |
|---|---|---|
| 10/20/22<br><br>Poisonous messages | Father suggested Mother's parents be put on supervised visitation. Claims they "don't know how to take care of children properly" and "are mean" and have badmouthed them to kids intermittently. | Binder tab 5, p. 38-54 (includes the parenting app Our Family Wizard, chain, multiple photos of children enjoying annual family reunions and parties together) |
| 12/21-Present<br><br>Blocking Contact & Comms | Father sends back unopened Christmas cards and gifts during the years he has the holiday with the kids. Says he deserves "uninterrupted" time, and "gifts are an unfair distraction." Kids have expressed sadness and confusion. | Binder tab 6, p 11-13 (OFW messages, photos of returned cards and gifts) |
| 1/23, 4/23, 9/23<br><br>Blocking Contact & Comms | Father coaches son's baseball with another child's parent and keeps taking Mother off the email list, so she has missed several of the child's games—the child reported that "Dad said you were too busy." | Binder tab, p4 (OFW messages, copies of emails from coaches) |
| 3/24<br><br>Erasing / replacing | Father baptized his Jewish daughter without any consent or even a conversation. Has secretly enrolled her in confirmation classes. Also sent her back to Mother wearing a cross. | Binder tab 8, p 24-39 (Photos, baptism invite, copy of agreement stating joint legal decision making). |

| cont'd.... | | |
|---|---|---|
| 5/2/24<br><br>Minimizing authority | Son reported Father saying, "Mom's rules don't matter, I have primary custody, so I'm in charge." | Binder tab 2, p 3 (Timeline, OFW message memorializing incident, no response received) |
| 6/15/24<br><br>Fostering dependency | Father refused to allow the teen child to attend school trip with the entire grade to Yellowstone Park because "he's more comfortable at home with me, and couldn't handle it." | Binder tab 4, p 6-9 (School trip description, multiple emails) |

Attorney Leona Krasner says you want to get as much proof as you can possibly include and "throw the kitchen sink at the other side." She urges people to state the violation, ask for sanctions in the form of fines, prison time, counsel fees, and changes to custody because of how serious this is. She said that you need to come at this strongly, or else a judge isn't going to pay attention. Getting everyone lined up immediately so they're ready to go is what Charles Jamieson calls taking the "*blitzkrieg*" defense approach to effectively deal with false allegations, which play a big role in how alienation cases begin.

### One Place to Start: A Clear, Concise Narrative

You want to tie it all together: your narrative of the problem, what's happened (with proof), and your well-reasoned, focused solution …what you're asking for and why the court should award it.

The strongest cases are demonstrably aligned with the values of the family court, as expressed in:

- The best interest factors applicable in your jurisdiction
- The factors in parental alienation
- Possibly the Children's Bill of Rights
- Anything you know about how your particular judge has handled cases like yours in the past

If you're defending yourself against false claims of parental alienation, the best thing you can do is show your nearly superhuman efforts to support your ex's relationship with your child through your documented actions and direct communications.

## The Patterns Will Emerge

There's no way around it: building a court case, whether you are trying to show your ex's alienating behaviors or that their claims that you're the alienator are without merit, is a lot of work. It takes diligent effort over an extended period of time to show these patterns. The good news is that it doesn't take any special skill. And, if your ex feels like the rules don't apply to them, as many alienators do, they're probably giving you a lot to work with on a regular basis.

## Questions for Reflection

1. Consider Dr. Amy Baker's Five-Factor Model. For each factor (how your child avoids you, your prior positive relationship, absence of abuse/neglect on your part, your ex's alienating behaviors, and your child's behavioral manifestations). What specific evidence do you currently

have, and what additional documentation might you need to gather?
2. If you had to present your case to a judge tomorrow, what would be your three strongest pieces of evidence that alienating behavior is occurring?
3. What would be your specific request for relief, and how might it help?

## CHAPTER 9

# BUILDING YOUR TEAM: CHOOSING THE RIGHT PROFESSIONALS

> *"People who haven't had to wrestle with deeply painful, unsolvable issues may not have the capacity to help support you. They have a smaller experiential vocabulary."*
>
> —Dr. Josh Coleman, Psychologist

**Your Support Team**

We often talk about how these situations are so crazy that it takes a team to navigate them and get yourself and your children to the other side as unscathed as possible.

Long before *Been There Got Out*, when we first met, we had no way of knowing that we were each only at the beginning of our respective legal marathons. The details of our divorces were different. Lisa's was more of a long slog that lasted nearly a decade, mostly post-judgment, and the issues were primarily financial. Chris' was a three-year bloodbath followed by intermittent flare-ups, and the fight was mostly focused on custody. They were both exhausting in their own ways.

Whether you're involved with the legal system or not, dealing with parental alienation is every bit as exhausting as a protracted high-conflict divorce; it's just a war being fought in a different environment. The common thread is that **you've acquired your own personal terrorist who will stop at nothing** to continue to exert power over you, using whatever means are available, be it courts, money, or the children you share.

The people you surround yourself with during this ordeal are essential. But it's equally important to make smart choices about who not to have in your inner circle. Having reasonable expectations of each person in your informal, or "natural," support network is necessary, so keep the following in mind:

1. **You're going to need a diverse skill set.** Let the people in your life help you in the ways that they can, and don't expect more. Sometimes, it's enough just to have small talk over a cup of coffee; not everyone needs the whole story. Even if your situation is always on your mind, you need distractions; more importantly, you need normalcy wherever you can find it.

2. **Support can come from unexpected sources** - not necessarily your closest lifelong contacts. Chris reconnected with two friends while he was in the thick of it; one whom he'd stayed in casual contact with since college, and the other whom he hadn't spoken with since high school, other than saying "hi" on Facebook. They were incredibly supportive early on (thanks so much, Jill and Jeannie!). Sometimes, a person outside your immediate circle has a more distant vantage point that can offer a valuable perspective.

3. **Your family and friends are likely not trained mental health professionals.** They're probably not going to have solutions, and the most they'll be able to offer is a caring ear. But this alone can be priceless.

The people you trust the most are the people to keep closest to you, but try not to wear them out; we see that a lot, and we've even had people hire us to help ease the stress being put on their relationships with new partners or family from dealing with everything.

### The Advocates You Want

In his book, *Don't Alienate the Kids*, Bill Eddy talks about what he calls *positive and negative advocates*. Negative advocates may "absorb the emotions of the high-conflict person," and usually communicate with a lot of emotional intensity, Eddy explained in an interview with us. They do nothing to help the situation and often fan the flames of conflict.

Eddy says that positive advocates are people who help, have an optimistic perspective, and will encourage productive behavior. Family members who want to truly assist will not be blaming your ex, but perhaps pointing you to resources, offering encouragement, and boosting your self-esteem. The simple takeaway is that negative advocates reinforce negative behavior, and positive advocates reinforce helpful behavior.

Your ex may be actively recruiting people to take their side, maybe even your own friends or family members. Your approach can be different. You don't need people to take sides, but instead to support you in seeking a positive resolution to some thorny issues.

As you seek your own positive advocates, look for people capable of supporting you, your ex, and/or your children with encouragement, caring, information, and ideas, rather than blame and demands for aggressive action. Positive advocates generally display an ability to:

- Avoid making assumptions
- Be flexible in their thinking
- Investigate problems and gather ideas, rather than rush to a single solution
- Provide support and information
- Remain pragmatic and not get caught up in the surrounding emotions
- Avoid taking sides and see the good and bad qualities in both you and your ex

**Ready... Set...**

As widespread as alienation is, it's still the vast minority of total divorces and separations. Thus, judges don't see a lot of these cases, and you should not assume they are well-versed in the subject. Charles Jamieson stresses that having experts who are familiar with alienation and the pressure on children in situations like these is a way for you **to educate the court about the reality of these situations.**

Unfortunately, fighting takes money. Jamieson says that sometimes your best bet is having an investigator who's both an expert in mental health and custody evaluation. An in-depth look at your case by experts with multiple skill sets can additionally provide a 360-degree view of all the allegations and influences. Even though it takes time, if you can get all of these in place, you have the best chance at having the truth prevail, because your ex certainly isn't going to come to court and acknowledge what they've done.

## Behind Closed Doors

New York City attorney Arique Dross acknowledges that part of why these cases are so hard to prove is that the conduct occurs behind closed doors.

Another thorny issue is that so much depends on the age of the child. Sometimes the court won't allow a young child to testify in open court, but will instead have something called a **"Lincoln hearing"** (also called in camera), during which private testimony will be allowed between the child and the judge, without any parents or attorneys, so that the child can present their wishes and/or concerns.

However, when damage has been done, the child may just parrot what has been fed to them by your ex. This is why it's so important to get mental health professionals involved to evaluate the entire family, so that they can come up with conclusions based on detailed investigations and evidence, which should help the court make more informed decisions.

## What Kind of Mental Health Professionals Should I Use?

According to Charles Jamieson, two types of people generally get involved in evaluating cases like these. The first is a clinical professional who will generally accept what a patient says at face value and not go deeper into determining the validity of specific allegations. Most attorneys who specialize in cases like these recommend instead to get a forensic evaluator to check for specific behaviors indicating that your ex has been turning your child against you. A forensic evaluator uses more detailed investigative procedures and sticks with very specific guidelines. Not every psychologist will be knowledgeable in this area! You want someone who has devoted themselves to this topic, if possible.

## The Right Questions to Ask

It can feel overwhelming to have to build a legal case and gather a team of professionals together against the backdrop of all of your own emotional turmoil. Knowing the right questions to ask is a great place to start, and here are a few to consider when selecting an evaluator:

1. Have you evaluated cases involving a parent turning children against another parent post-separation?
2. What methods do you use to determine if this behavior is caused by the other parent or not?
3. Have you ever found parental alienation to exist in any of the cases that you have examined?
4. What type did you find (mild, moderate, or severe)?
5. How were you able to determine what type it was?
6. After making a conclusion, what recommendations or intervention programs did you have to fix the situation?
7. What specific recommendations did you make for the targeted parent (a parent in a similar situation to yours)?
8. What specific recommendations did you make for the child who had been affected?
9. How do we know how to tell if something has been effective?
10. Can you share any success stories?

A degree in psychology is no guarantee that a professional will have sufficient expertise to manage cases like these, and it's imperative that the people working with you and your child have both training and experience in this specific area of domestic violence, including knowledge of protocols in child forensic interviewing.

## How Do I Choose the Right Counselor For Our Family?

According to Bill Eddy, who was also a social worker before becoming an expert in high-conflict divorce and resolution, these are a few things to look for when selecting a counselor:

1. Ask what experience they have with high-conflict families. Eddy notes that it's good if they have had experience working with personality disorders, as well as training in DBT (dialectical behavior therapy). Even though this type of therapy was designed for borderline personality disorder, they will certainly be more likely to understand the kind of dynamics you and/or your child are experiencing.
2. Find someone experienced in alienation and who is also able to work collaboratively with other professionals.
3. Make sure you feel their sense of empathy, rather than judgment. Remember, this is going to be an intimate relationship, and you need to feel comfortable with whoever you work with.

Additionally, here are some more specific questions to consider asking when looking for a mental health professional to help your family.

1. **What are the goals of counseling, and how can they be specifically achieved?** Does the counselor use any

particular methods? If so, how might they be applied to what you're looking to accomplish?

2. **If a child doesn't want to go, are we going to force them to do it?** Should they be allowed to go at their own pace, knowing that this is being influenced by the other parent?

3. **How can we stay resolution-focused and avoid the "blame game"?** Talking about the past matters to some extent, but at what point is it possible to come up with a plan moving forward?

4. **How will the counseling be structured?** What are the logistics? Are sessions always done in person? Virtually? Do parents and children meet together or have their own separate counseling sessions? Should your ex be involved with either the child or directly with the counselor?

5. **Will the counselor be able to make decisions regarding access schedules?** How much influence will this have on a more permanent parenting plan and custody itself?

6. **How much decision-making will be made by the court?** Or will individual details be handled by either the counselor or some type of parenting coordinator or other court-appointed professional chosen by the parties themselves?

7. **How will the team of professionals work together to communicate if and how goals are being achieved?** If more than one person is involved, how often will the group meet to discuss, and what might your responsibilities be throughout the process?

8. **Is there any kind of timeline associated with this plan?** And how long will it take to get there, or to measure progress?

9. **What are the visible indicators of success?** How will you know whether therapy is effective or not

As children in these situations can feel that they are prohibited from having a loving relationship with you, Eddy strongly encourages that your ex participate in counseling with your child, which may be difficult to make happen. He also recommends that counseling should include giving options rather than rigidly directing. If the therapist can come from the angle of helping your ex make decisions, rather than making decisions for them, they are less likely to be blamed (and/or fired!)

## What If My Kid is Being Coached?

Former sheriff, Child Protective Services worker, and attorney Evynne Fair shared with us how she was able to tell if a kid was being coached by a parent to report things that were not necessarily true. She talked with us about a case involving a young girl who came in and was very detailed in her descriptions about things that had happened, as though someone had rehearsed it with her.

Fair said that it's normal for people to forget certain moments in time, especially when they've been traumatized, so when someone remembers every single detail from an event that supposedly occurred years ago, it raises a red flag of suspicion. This doesn't mean that we automatically disbelieve a child, but that other steps must be taken before moving forward in filing anything, including further investigation and interviews. But how can professionals tell? Former Canadian children's lawyer Nicolle Kopping-Pavars says that there are three main factors professionals use to determine if a child has been coached:

1. **Consistency.** Is the child saying the same thing again and again, or does the story change?

2. **Independence**. Does the story stay the same no matter which parent brings them to a meeting?
3. **Appropriate language**. Is the child's vocabulary natural? For example, a seven-year-old saying that her dad had an "inappropriate reaction" does not sound like a typical expression for a child of that age. Although some children certainly are advanced, can they explain what they mean, or are they just parroting something they've heard?

Many people we work with worry about the fact that their child even needs an attorney. Kopping-Pavars found that managing a parent's expectations was a large part of her job, and making it very clear what her role was had to happen early on. Sometimes evaluators are pressured by a parent to address questions that they feel should be asked; instead, it's more open-ended. She feels that the child should take the lead in telling her what matters most.

Children pick up on your anxiety. If your kid is nervous, a good children's lawyer might allow you to come in for a meet-and-greet and ask questions. Try to show your child that you trust their attorney. And don't panic unnecessarily! If you are involved as a parent, then there's nothing to worry about regarding what your child is going to say to their lawyer, notes Kopping-Pavars.

## Do No (More) Harm

Psychologist Dr. Liz Stilwell works with many difficult cases, and these land in her lap generally after an investigation by Child Protective Services, an evaluation by other professionals, or some kind of determination by the court. Acting as a therapist is a significant role, so she wants to understand as much as possible about what's going on with any allegations to understand proper treatment. During her intake with everyone involved, if she feels uncertain about the validity of allegations, she may refer the family back to the evaluation process.

## Why Kids Need Therapy

No matter how hard you try to shield them from conflict and court proceedings, kids pick up on everything. Their world has been upended, and they're now trying to make sense of it all. This very emotionally trying time in your own life will impact them, says Stilwell. There is a consensus that kids need therapy before, during, and after divorce, especially in high-conflict situations. However, don't rush your kid to a therapist with the idea that they will be a witness to help you in your case. Irish play therapist Edel Lawlor says that therapy for children during litigation has to be approached with extraordinary caution, and sometimes may not even be a good idea. "When parents are in toxic conflict with each other, you know they will do what they can for a child to say a certain thing to a professional. So, therefore, how can the child's therapy be therapeutic?"

**Children need to have their own place to heal** and to know that whatever they say will not upset their mother or father. This can be tricky when considering your child's therapist as a potential witness.

As adults in therapy, we know that we can say whatever we want. But imagine if, after revealing highly sensitive, private information, your therapist then announced that they were going to write a report for a judge regarding everything you just said, and share it with the people you talked about. How would you feel in a situation like that?

A scenario like this in your child's life could significantly impact their attitude about therapy in the future, if an early experience with a therapist was a betrayal.

Lawlor argues that "protection is paramount" and recommends that a therapist not write a detailed report for a judge. Instead, just have them provide confirmation that sessions were attended. Of course, if anything comes up in therapy where there's a concern regarding child protection, she is compelled to intervene; otherwise, therapy should be a safe place, where the relationship can remain private and sacred.

When she works with children whose parents are in litigation, she makes sure to first ask the child if there is anything they want her to tell the judge.

Psychologist Dr. David Marcus notes that when he deals with narcissistic parents who insist they're right and the other person's at fault, he has to be able to say, "If you keep telling this stuff to your kids, I'm going to tell the judge." Otherwise, a parent has no motivation to change bad behavior.

Dr. Marcus typically builds rapport with his young clients by talking to them about whatever's important to them, and letting them define the word *important*. He says that although it usually starts off as something to do with "Minecraft," children generally will get into the family dynamics eventually. He does not like to say, "Tell me about your mom and dad," or "Tell me what your mom/dad said," because that scares kids who feel like they don't want to get a parent in trouble. By just talking about what's important to them, a lot comes out, especially through artwork, which can say so much.

- When children draw pictures with one parent looming over the other, it signifies how they perceive the power dynamic in the house, noting who is subordinate.
- Kids depicted with big eyes demonstrate their own hypervigilance.

- Houses with no chimneys show no sense or warmth, or grounding.
- Homes with no windows imply a child being closed off.

All of these images help him learn what's going on inside a child's head, and what he needs to talk to parents about.

**Choosing the Right Therapist For Yourself**

If your kid is going to a wonderful therapist and learning the right strategies to manage his or her stress, anxiety, or social issues, but then goes back home to parents who don't understand how to monitor and alter their own behaviors, it's useless, says mental health professional Lauren Barnett, founder of Family Consultants of Westport.

Parents don't think we're part of the problem, but we have to learn the same tools. Any improvements that we make are going to benefit our child. Bottom line: Why not get some mental health help for yourself?

The best indicator of successful therapy is the therapeutic alliance, or relationship between you and your counselor, and Barnett is what we think of as a therapist "matchmaker" who can help find the perfect mental health professional for you.

She starts the process by first learning about who you are as a person, and at the same time, she's getting information on mental health concerns. She encourages you to think about the following before shopping for a therapist:

- Who was your favorite teacher, coach, babysitter, or camp counselor?
- How did they motivate you? What made you want to show up for that person?

- What techniques or ideas worked in the past to help you get through something?
- What kind of person do you tend not to connect with? Why?

Thinking about the answers to these questions is relaxing, empowering, and will encourage you to think differently about therapy. Of course, this is about much more than just showing up and sitting in a room together; you have to be ready to do the work.

## My Attorney Doesn't Do Alienation

According to attorney Ashish Joshi, if your lawyer doesn't have meaningful experience with the topic of alienation, they need to talk to lawyers who are specialists. Arguing these cases requires a very specific set of data and skills to litigate effectively. Attorneys who understand extreme situations are few and far between. Remember, your lawyer's job is to be your advocate and to communicate effectively. But it's also important for them to be schooled in what they are addressing.

The reason many cases involving a child being turned against a healthy, loving parent fail is that an inexperienced attorney ignored advice from an expert, was ill-prepared, and failed to use effective legal strategies. Spending the money for your lawyer to consult with an experienced attorney in this field for a couple of hours might be the difference between winning and losing in court.

## Choosing The Right Attorney

If you already have a lawyer, you can skip this part. But if you're just starting to address this issue, you want to try to find someone who really understands and cares about cases like yours. The right attorney should take the time to make you feel heard and then explain what the game plan is.

The following are some questions to ask during an initial consultation:

1. **How do you plan on addressing the family dynamics, considering that my children have been turned against me?** We hope your lawyer makes clear how urgent it is not to let your situation languish.
2. **How can we effectively educate the court on what's going on?** Make sure your lawyer has a clear strategy and execution plan.
3. **How have you handled cases like mine in the past?** This is our favorite question, and it will reveal if the lawyer has listened to what you've said and can easily provide a couple of ideas that have worked.
4. **Can you share any success stories?** Hopefully, the prior question will have prompted at least one success story; ask for any other cases they handled where a child was effectively reconnected with an alienated parent.

When you sense that your lawyer is your ally as well as an advocate, you will be in a better mental state, and you can help them put together an action plan and collaborate by organizing targeted documentation so they can prepare to litigate more effectively.

## How Should I Handle Expert Witnesses or Evaluators?

Here are some things to consider when looking for an expert who may investigate or testify in your case:

1. **Has this person already been qualified as an expert in this or a related field?** Have they ever given testimony

before on this topic, and was it ever precluded or excluded by a court for whatever reason?
2. **Make sure the expert is well-educated.** They should have at least a master's or doctoral degree from an accredited educational institution in social work, psychology, or psychiatry.
3. **Test their knowledge.** Do they understand the dynamics of alienation, estrangement, and personality disorders, which are common among rejecting parents?
4. **What peer-reviewed literature are they aware of?** How do they keep up with the latest information on these topics?
5. **What, if any, educational or training programs by qualified experts on the topic of alienation or estrangement have they completed?**
6. **What knowledge do they have of the various theories around alienation, and how those theories are understood and applied in your jurisdiction?** Are they familiar with interventions that specific courts have ordered when provided with solid evidence that alienation is happening?
7. **Has this expert published any information themselves on the topic?** Keep in mind that not everyone may have done this, but it's certainly helpful!
8. **Have they ever presented information on this topic to their peers?** What networks of mental health or legal professionals regard them highly, if any?

Having someone on your team with a medical background can save you enormous amounts of time, money, and energy because their skills can hone in on information you might not even think to look for. A legal nurse is a fairly new profession, and can help you put together a strong case when it comes to dealing with the medical and mental health issues so often at the forefront of these situations. Legal nurse Tara Zacharzuk-Marciano finds appropriate peer-reviewed literature and expert witnesses, both of which can strengthen your case.

## Police Involvement

It can be immensely frustrating that the police cannot physically remove your child from your ex's home when they are not complying with your agreement or court order. The police generally do not like to get too involved; however, if you have a court order, at the very least, they should be able to make a report as well as tell your ex that they are in violation by not bringing back your child.

We wish they could throw your ex in jail, which we've rarely seen happen, but know that with the written report, you have strong documentation for when you do go back to court, and we have numerous clients who successfully used police reports as evidence to strengthen a custody case.

## Supervised Visitation Can Be a Good Thing

Attorney Charles Jamieson says that decades ago, he was outraged when anyone even suggested that his innocent client be required to go on supervised visitation. It felt like complying was an admission of wrongdoing. Over time, his opinion changed because he saw that supervised visitation could be used to his client's advantage.

Showing off your amazing parenting skills to a supervisor can be a great opportunity to create a powerful witness who is able to refute all of your ex's allegations that the kids don't want to see you or are being harmed by your behavior. Supervised visits can be quite expensive, and sometimes people prefer to use a friend or family member for convenience and cost. However, a professional supervisor can testify about your parenting, your kid's response to you, and hopefully that they see nothing wrong with your parenting skills and that your child is acting normally towards you.

A supervisor may also witness your ex's behavior during exchanges. We know that disordered people cannot always hold it together, and often they will act out in front of the visitation center staff or even the supervisor. This is gold, according to Jamieson, who believes the cost of supervised visitation is well worth it.

One of our clients' exes started saying that their daughter would not get out of the car anymore after our client got more time for his visitations. There had been no prior issues with her being fearful, and there was documentation that every visit had gone well. The supervisor at the center was then able to report to the court how his ex was interfering with the court order by making transitions difficult.

Professional supervisor Diana Canas notes that most people are on their best behavior during supervised visitation when it's a couple of hours, and that's why the goal is to increase the time and expand the geography of where a supervised visit can take place. As the hours increase, she likes to try moving into the community and then to your home to see you in your natural environment. How do you deal with real-life situations? Are you able to handle the most stressful moments of the day, like getting the kids to school when you're also trying to feed them and get ready for work yourself? Those are the kinds of things a supervisor needs to keep an eye on. Most people are embarrassed to be out in the community with a supervisor, but Canas stresses that she tries to blend in. Depending on the vibe the kid is giving, she may talk to them or not, but her overall goal is to minimize stress on the child.

## Choosing a Supervisor

Canas urges you to shop around for the right supervisor, just as you would a car, and see what they have to offer. Some of what you might consider ahead of time:

1. **Make a connection.** Is the supervisor willing to offer time for you to meet with them before hiring? It's important to see if there's a connection first.
2. **We tell our kids, "Don't go with strangers."** It's a great idea for a supervisor to meet with both parents before the visits to show that Mom or Dad knows them; this helps make sure your child feels like it's ok, so therefore no one is a stranger. If the supervisor can take a few minutes to interact with your child before having them get in a car or go somewhere together, it can make a big difference.
3. **If your ex is the one being supervised:** Don't tell your child that you're waiting outside in the parking lot in case it doesn't go well! Kids feel everything, and you don't want them to pick up on whatever anxiety you have.

On top of everything else, we want to ensure that your child is prepared for supervised visits. Kids, like everyone else, do better when they know the routine, so it's important to talk to them ahead of time. If you can, let them know where they're going, like to a park, and mention what they might do afterward, like have dinner. With older kids, you can say that mom and dad are having a bit of a hard time right now, but it's important for them to spend time with each of you. Be conscious of your body language and try to act as calmly as possible so that your child feels less anxious and knows that the supervisor, whom they may have already met, will also be there to help take care of them.

## Questions for Reflection

When we talk with our clients about taking strategic oversight of their case, we ask them to take the lead. Both skill and chemistry matter here. You get to pick the players, your advocates, but you're also responsible for keeping everyone in their lane and moving in the right direction.

1. Looking at your current support network, who are your "positive advocates" versus "negative advocates"?
2. What changes could you make to surround yourself with more helpful influences?
3. Based on the questions provided for selecting evaluators and therapists, which professionals in your current team (if any) may not have the right expertise for your situation?
4. What might you be able to do to either change things or adapt your own behavior to make up for any shortcomings of your team?

## CHAPTER 10

## NAILING YOUR PRESENTATION

*"One of the surefire ways to tank a forensic evaluation is for a lawyer to counsel his client to be him or herself while meeting with the evaluator."*

—Ashish Joshi, Attorney

### Con Artists in Court

Psychologist and alienation expert Dr. Steven G. Miller spent decades studying the effects of parental alienation and found that alienating parents often present with what he calls the "**Four C's**": cool, calm, charming, and convincing. Master manipulators are wonderful at managing impressions, and the court, especially the family court, gives them a stage on which to perform.

In contrast, targeted parents, like you, tend to manifest the "**Four A's**": anxious, agitated, angry, and afraid. People who are not experts in domestic violence issues can misinterpret these cues and may become convinced that your ex's narrative is valid—which can be catastrophic. You're dealing with so much: fury over your ex's repeated violations of your parenting plan, heartbreak over your child's rejection, and frustration with the professionals in the family court's ecosystem. It's entirely understandable.

With all of these strong emotions swirling around while you try to operate in a totally foreign environment where so much hangs in the balance, it is essential to get the support and education you need to present properly in and out of the courtroom. Your compelling narrative needs to receive the attention and weight it deserves.

## I Need Justice NOW!

We imagine you're champing at the bit to talk to someone with the authority to address all of the damage that your ex continues to do. But going into court, a custody evaluation, or any situation where you'll make an impact with "guns blazing" is not the optimal mindset for making a great first impression.

We meet many people who say, "My evaluator doesn't care that my ex is an abuser!" They may even suspect bias or corruption. More often than not, the real problem is a lack of understanding of the factors that court professionals care about. We want to make sure that, from this moment on, you don't make the same mistakes and play right into your ex's portrayal of you as difficult to deal with. It all boils down to being strategic about how you present yourself. You should come across as the best co-parent ever, no matter how impossible the circumstances seem.

## Don't Push Too Far

During a support group session, one of our clients was expressing deep frustration that the GAL assigned to their case had not listened to her perspective. He had given her multiple opportunities to share her feelings and provide reasons for what she wanted, but had nonetheless suggested a bit more parenting time for her ex in the form of an additional overnight.

Even though she would have still had a favorable arrangement, she was upset and kept calling her lawyer, who, in turn, became frustrated with her and less responsive to her messages. With her court date upcoming, at which the GAL was scheduled to present his recommendations, she shared with the group how she planned to explain again, this time to the judge (since the GAL "didn't get it"), how abusive her ex had been, and how unconscionable it would be to give that monster even another minute with their daughter. Those weren't her exact words, but they might as well have been.

The other clients in our group urged her to back off and let her ex have the extra overnight that the GAL supported. Sometimes, it's better to live to fight another day when conditions aren't favorable. It was clear that her narrative wasn't landing with the GAL, and also becoming apparent that she was starting to irritate everyone. She aggressively pushed her agenda again in court, explaining how important it was to "protect" her daughter, criticizing the aspects of the GAL's report that she didn't agree with. The only real surprise to us was that she didn't lose more decisively than she did. The judge admonished her for her own alienating behaviors, and it's probably going to take years for her to rehabilitate her image in that court. She's lucky her ex wasn't going harder.

If this case is an example of a "broken" system, it's luckily something you can understand and navigate. You are allowed to feel big emotions, but your behavior must always reflect respect toward the court and legal process. You are allowed to worry about your kids and view your ex as a monster. Just don't show it to anyone who has a say in your case!

## False Allegations & Credibility

False accusations are a given in our community, and they often occur at the worst times, especially at the beginning of a case, before you even realize exactly what and who you're up against. Many of our clients have had restraining orders filed against them without justification, or had a difficult ex file a(nother) child abuse report because they sensed they were losing, and knew what an effective distraction this could be. The court focuses on the most immediate issues, which can tend to further delay justice, especially during heated custody battles.

Of course, false accusations can spring up anywhere, not just in court. Your ex may make them to mandated reporters, like your child's pediatrician or school nurse, who have no choice but to report them to the authorities. Many of us have an innate belief that truth and justice will ultimately prevail. In our world, that's far from a given.

Custody battles are so subjective that they often come down to what attorney Charles Jamieson calls a *battle of imagery*. Opposing counsel attempts to make you look like someone who might have abused your child. They exaggerate harmless incidents and blatantly lie. Judges sometimes believe false accusations with no proof, maybe because your ex somehow seems more credible. And it doesn't help that people like them always seem to hire bully lawyers who enable their nonsense.

Things can go sideways quickly. If you defend yourself too vigorously, you might appear guilty. If you don't defend yourself strongly enough, you might appear... guilty. It's a fine line. And if you can't control your emotions and lash out at your ex in frustration, their lawyer presents your rant to the court, burying you further.

Jamieson says that the system sometimes takes an "axiomatic" or "stereotypical" position: no one is believed because it's just assumed that everyone lies (which stems from the problem that family courts generally don't hold people accountable for perjury to the extent that other types of courts do).

Another challenge when it comes to false allegations is the understandably careful approach many judges default to: erring on the side of caution. No judge wants to be responsible for giving a child to someone facing serious abuse allegations and then have something terrible happen. So, while you're clearing your name, you might not even see your kids, or you might be put on supervised visitation. There is no foolproof method for dealing with false accusations, but everything in family court starts with your image, in the eyes of the judge and other influential players. The more they like you, the more likely they are to believe you. So, make sure you know how to behave in court, how to communicate with your ex, and what the court cares about.

### Getting it Right from the Start CPS Workers.

How can you make the best impression under the worst of circumstances? Different jurisdictions have different names for agencies chartered to investigate reports involving the welfare of children. "Child Protective Services" (CPS) is common (and the name we use in this book), but it could be DCS, DCFS, or something similar; Cafcass performs this role in the UK and Canada.

CPS is commonly called into our clients' lives to investigate claims that a child's safety or well-being is at risk. The first thing you want to know about any of these organizations is that the bar for "abuse" is set very high. They routinely see children in situations where the conditions are deplorable and the abuse or neglect is obvious. It takes a lot to get a "substantiated" report when claims of abuse are filed.

### CPS: Making the Best Impression

If your ex, or someone acting on something your ex said, has made a false accusation against you to Child Protective Services, we want you to approach the process not with suspicion, which will immediately put an evaluator on defense, but instead with a sense of curiosity. Not easy! According to attorney and former CPS worker Evynne Fair, you can't just sit back and expect the truth to come out. She has seen far too many situations where fear and panic set in in the face of false allegations, along with a sense that no one is going to believe you. When you haven't done anything wrong and are accused of horrific things, it's normal to think, How dare you say that I did this? Fair has seen far too many people make the mistake of texting or calling their ex and getting into an argument, saying things in the heat of the moment that might not look good later. Be careful what you say when you're angry—no popping off!

Here are some ideas from Evynne Fair, on how to handle yourself properly if you become the subject of an investigation:

1. If you have an attorney, reach out and let them know what's going on as soon as possible.
2. As frustrating as it can be, cooperate with the CPS worker. Let them do what they need to for the investigation. This is their job, and they have to investigate all reports based on the allegations.
3. If you feel really uncomfortable, and if it's allowed in your state, try to have a third person present, like your attorney, especially during a scheduled home visit.
4. Absolutely do not lash out at the worker. They did not file the case! Be as calm and cooperative as possible.

We know how terrifying this can be. In our experience, many of these false accusations result in reports that are unfounded. Try to have faith that the truth of the matter will come out.

## First Impressions

There are plenty of times we all want to scream from the rooftops, "How can you not see it?" The last thing we want is for you to insult a professional's intelligence or appear emotionally dysregulated yourself. We understand, truly. When you're in a custody battle with a former partner who's alienating your child from you, it feels like life and death. It's terrifying to know that whoever this professional is will spend only a bit of time digging into what's going on in your family and then make a recommendation that may be *the* deciding factor.

As we share regularly in our social media content, understanding the decorum of the legal process is not just for the actual courthouse when you're in front of a judge. Conducting yourself respectfully at every step and especially when you interact with any officer of the court is a basic requirement for navigating the legal process successfully. None of these people is there to hear you vent about your horrible ex. A huge part of etiquette is knowing your place in the pecking order: the very bottom. Don't be a know-it-all during an appointment with an evaluator or bring in a pile of literature on parental alienation and try to school them on what it means. Also, expect this to be a dialogue. An evaluator should not just sit back and collect the facts you present. Don't be offended when they try to confirm what you are saying. Remember, they'll talk with your ex also, who is surely going to paint a false picture of what's been going on. You want the evaluator to be skeptical and curious to know more, and although their skepticism may make you feel uncomfortable, you want them to question.

## Strategic Communication with Professionals

One of our clients' exes abandoned their son, going as far as signing away his parental rights. Years later, he changed his mind and started a custody battle that had been going on for quite a while by the time we met her. As usual, he and his lawyer were throwing everything at her, including false allegations of parental alienation.

The court's commitment to the core value of having two parents involved is a powerful one. Although their son's therapist cited reasons for opposing reconciliation, our client's ex prevailed in court, and the decision was made to select a reunification therapist. One of the experts involved had a reputation for taking alienation claims seriously, which, of course, terrified our client. She wanted to know what to ask the reunification therapist before hiring him, and sent us a draft of her email. It included reasonable questions, such as how long the therapist had been in practice, but some of them might have come across as confrontational. Here's the original version:

> "I reached out to your office last week because I'm currently involved in a custody battle with my son's father, and we are seeking to align on a reunification therapist. My ex recommended you, but I first need to ensure that you would be a great support for our complex case. I am curious as to your experience in working with cases regarding allegations of alienation, narcissism, domestic violence, etc., and am interested to learn more about how you've navigated through them. It's important that my son has healthy access to both parents and feels supported wherever he is."

Although this was a good try, we definitely did not want this first letter to create the wrong impression, and noticed some "red flag" words that might have sent the wrong signals. We took them out (*custody battle, I first need, alienation, narcissism, it's important that my son has...*), and after a session together, this was the "tweaked" letter that was sent out:

> "I reached out to your office last week because our son's dad recommended you as a reunification therapist. I'd love to know more about your practice to understand how this works, and especially how I can support our son throughout this process. Thank you for your time and consideration. Please feel free to reach out if you have any questions or need additional information."

Note the more positive tone, the cooperative nature of being willing to go along with the process, and the gentle "I'd love to know more about your practice" and "How can I support our son throughout this process?" And always use "our" son or daughter, never "my." The focus is squarely on her child, rather than her fears, and this edited version oozes confidence and security.

## The Evaluator

Custody evaluators review the same documents and evidence that you bring to court, but have more time to dig deeper and form an opinion on what's happening beneath the surface; that's their job. They also may be more open to considering submissions like recordings, which judges tend to dislike.

If your ex is making claims of domestic violence or that you were never around when your child was growing up, you will need to show evidence to the contrary.

Attorney Ashish Joshi says that when choosing your collateral, or witnesses, consider people who can help validate the fact that you have a history of a good, healthy relationship with your child, and can verify that you did nothing to deserve the rejection you're experiencing.

## No Big Binders

One thing we see people do, especially before our first conversation with them, is go into an evaluation with a huge binder of evidence showing what a terrible parent their ex is. This flies in the face of court values, specifically the best interest factor, that they would like to see both of you supporting the child's relationship with each other. If you walk into an evaluation leading off with how bad your child's other parent is, you are likely to ruin things for yourself.

Conflict resolution expert Bill Eddy recommends that when you communicate with court professionals, you use "simple" language with somewhat emotional words. Here are three "court-approved" categories to organize your evidence around. Show how your ex:

- "Undermines my parenting"
- "Presents false statements to the court"
- "Engages in emotional abuse toward our child"

With strong supporting evidence and a dash of repetition, Eddy has found these themes very effective.

## Better Binders: An Accurate Picture

No evaluator wants to go through a pile of disorganized documentation and search for your evidence - remember, this is not a data dump. Your lawyer (and coaches like us) have the job of helping you put together a narrative to help "connect the dots" so that the relief you are seeking is well-positioned as an appropriate solution to the core problems that landed you in court.

Joshi recommends creating a tabulated binder that includes all of your materials, organized in the following manner:

1. A **comprehensive table of contents** that lists everything included, preferably organized chronologically. Each line should provide the location of the exhibit.
2. The **relevant date** of the event to which the piece of evidence applies.
3. A **brief description** of the exhibit.
4. An explanation as to **how the material is relevant** to the overall case.
5. After putting it all together, write a **cover letter** that briefly explains what's included and why.

By being meticulous and organized, you will be a pleasure to work with by making your evaluator's job easier. If their report later includes suggestions that you don't agree with, this information will help your attorney prepare to challenge those recommendations in court.

Make sure to include the big picture and not cherry-pick evidence that supports your narrative. For example, if you submit an email, include the entire chain to provide context and establish your credibility. And hold the other side to the same standards - don't passively accept their evidence if it's incomplete or lacks context.

## Up Your Credibility Game

Remember, your goal here is to help an investigator see the healthy and loving relationship that you once had with your child prior to separation from your ex. You want to demonstrate the baseline of a normal relationship to show that something *abnormal* has happened to disrupt it.

Do not be surprised if an evaluator asks you to share an extensive history of your relationship with your ex, and not just with your children. Be prepared to talk about what attracted you to your ex in the first place, details of your involvement as a parent from your child's birth until the separation, and what your role was in your child's life. Even if you were not the primary caregiver, you still deserve and have the right to a close relationship with your child!

The evaluator may also ask some version of:

- What are some specific complaints your children have against you?
- When did the complaints begin?
- More specifically, did they occur while you were still together with the child's other parent?

Be ready for the evaluator to go through any allegations from the other side. Try not to get defensive if it appears they're treating your ex's claims as valid. Remember, their job is to investigate, and they don't know you at all yet. You probably know what your ex is saying about you, and you need to be prepared to address their allegations with your testimony and whatever evidence you can provide. Bring documentation of your involvement in your kids' lives, such as school volunteer work, any coaching you might have done with your child's sports or activities, or your connection with their school.

Be ready to talk about — in detail and with enthusiasm — some of the **milestones** in your children's lives. For example, were you there for birthday parties, vacations, sporting events, school performances, and family celebrations? Again, storytelling can be powerful in painting a vivid picture in an evaluator's mind of how things are not the way they are being portrayed by your ex.

### Crack the Door Open

We sometimes meet people on the warpath, speaking in scathing language about all that their exes are doing. And a lot of times, we'll warn them: "If you present like Mama (or Papa) Bear, you'll get bitten by the system." Success in family court when parental alienation is happening or being alleged starts with understanding the values and expectations of the professionals you're likely to encounter along the way. Your presentation matters everywhere, not just in front of the judge. Act as if you were a politician running for office. You want to be *likable*. Your evidence and narrative are the steak; how you communicate and conduct yourself is the sizzle. If you stay composed, don't trash your ex, focus on the issues at hand and how they affect your children and your relationship with them, and align it all with the values of the family court, you'll give yourself the best chance at an outcome you can live with. For a lot of us, that means restoring or improving contact with our kids, even if it's just a little. Once that door is cracked open, your great parenting, genuine love, and your child's natural bond with you can have a chance to once again flourish.

## Questions for Reflection

1. Thinking about Dr. Steven Miller's "Four C's" versus "Four A's," how do you typically present in stressful situations?
2. What specific strategies can you practice to appear calmer and more credible when it matters most?
3. Using the UPS Framework, how would you introduce yourself, in your own words, to a new professional in your child's life (teacher, coach, therapist) to protect against potential negative influence from your ex?
4. What documentation do you currently have that shows your historical positive relationship with your child? What additional evidence could you gather to build credibility?

## CHAPTER 11

# PARENTING PLANS, RELIEF, & ENFORCEMENT

*"One of the worst things you can do is not enforce your parenting plan."*

—Billie Tarascio, Attorney

### The Court Finally Saw It!

Arizona attorney Billie Tarascio got a huge victory for a client whose child had been turned against her. The judge ruled that parental alienation had taken place, and, even more notably, wrote in the decision that the alienation "was a form of domestic violence."

In this particular case, the mother had gotten a DUI, and the father went to court and got primary physical and legal custody of their seven-year-old daughter. Because the parents lived about an hour apart and Mom had had her license suspended, she was unable to drive herself to visits. On top of that, the new order did not include any specific parenting time for her; like so many orders, this one was incomplete and didn't consider that the father was decidedly uncooperative.

Dad was supposed to accommodate parenting time, but for the next three years, he made it as difficult as he possibly could. He regularly badmouthed her mother and wouldn't answer or return Mom's calls, eventually blocking her number. He did the same with her family members who tried to contact their daughter, and even took her out of school.

It took these three years for Mom to put together a strong case and get a modification giving her more parenting time. The judge was so disgusted with the father's behavior that she found that it constituted parental alienation as well as domestic violence, and flipped custody: Mom became the primary custodial parent and was awarded tie-breaking authority for legal decision-making.

During the process, the daughter said in interviews that she wanted to stay with her father. However, the judge read between the lines in her ruling, noting that the child had been manipulated and alienated. Since then, the tables have turned completely, and now the girl doesn't want to see her father.

Despite all that had happened, Mom knows how important it is to still support their daughter's relationship with her father, and even though the child, now eleven, resists her father's visitation on the weekends, Mom is making sure that access time occurs.

How did the attorney win this case? Tarascio notes that this was such a severe case of alienation that the father had practically done the work for them. He had taken the child out of school, her grades had dropped, and he refused to share that information with the mother. For three years, he had effectively blocked contact and communication with their daughter by not allowing the other parent to see their child, and she had extensive phone records showing her attempts to call. And her family members testified about their attempts to make contact, all blocked by Dad. In the hands of an attorney skilled in prosecuting alienation cases, all of this painted a compelling picture.

## But I Should Be Flexible, Right?

Divorced parents are often put in a position where they want to do whatever they can to keep their children happy by being flexible about the schedule, especially as the kids get older. What might seem logical, like letting a kid not come to visit because they want to spend extra time with your ex that particular weekend, is not a good idea when kids are being poisoned against you. Also, if your ex is violating the court order, you want to make sure you can file for contempt. If you agreed to your child spending less time with you, that agreement takes away any legal basis for an argument.

If your ex is violating the parenting plan and nothing is done about it swiftly, the "status quo of repeated violations could suddenly become a new normal," according to Ashish Joshi. And it emboldens an abusive person to continue that behavior because they keep getting away with it.

## It Will (Probably) Take Time

In a perfect world, the family court would be immediately investigating, instead of waiting for trials that take months or years, because all that time can never be made up.

If a child has been coached to say that they were abused, a targeted parent could be stuck until the case plays out. Sometimes, people give up because they feel like they're fighting for so long, and progress, if any, is too slow.

In attorney Arique Dross' opinion, judges and referees are conservative and careful. They don't want to order visitation if a child is objecting, and often want to wait for an evaluator to weigh in, or at least have the opportunity to talk to a therapist before an order is issued. When large chunks of time pass without contact, it can start to feel like you're becoming a stranger to your own kid.

This is an excuse your ex might be using to delay further contact, when the goal should instead be to rebuild that relationship.

## Relief

Highly successful outcomes are more likely when they include **early intervention and preventative measures,** before violations become the new normal and the only remedy involves dragged-out, expensive litigation. So, how can this type of psychological abuse be stopped?

If bad behavior occurs without accountability, then nothing will change, and we must first figure out what to ask the court for. Here are some ideas:

- Financial sanctions
- Attorney fees and court costs
- Court-ordered makeup parenting time
- Changes in custody

## Dr. Baker's Baseball Analogy

One of the many hats Dr. Amy Baker has worn is that of an expert witness in alienation cases. In this capacity, she sees four hurdles you need to overcome to get a favorable outcome based on alienation, much like a baseball player has to reach four bases to score a run by getting home, and the goal is to get your child home.

To reach first base and even have a chance, the judge has to be at least open to the idea that it's possible for a child to be manipulated to reject a parent who does not deserve to be rejected (the difference between alienation and estrangement, from back in Chapter 1). As Dr. Baker says, "If the judge does not believe that, you will lose your case."

To get to second base, you need the judge to not only believe that parental alienation can happen, but that it's happening in your case. And that's where your excellent preparation and documentation are so crucial. Once the judge acknowledges that alienation is a real thing and that it's happening with your child, now you need to convince them that something needs to be done to reach third base. Judges are risk-averse, broadly speaking, as we discussed in the last chapter.

They can be hesitant to change anything, especially if it means a child might run away or harm themselves if they're wrong. If the child is doing well otherwise, why change anything? If the child is doing poorly, maybe struggling with anxiety or other issues, is it prudent to rock the boat now?

Now, you've built a great case, and the judge believes your ex is undermining your relationship with your child and wants to do something. But… what? You need to show the judge that the solution you have in mind is well-suited to addressing the problem to score the runner. What good would it do to have the judge rule in your favor, but order something that is doomed to be ineffective?

What you ask for has to be sufficient to address the problem, and you need guardrails, including deadlines, consequences, and follow-up for when your ex tries to sabotage the process.

## The Path to Relief

Ashish Joshi says several decisions have to be made before deciding on a resolution to seek so that remediation is ultimately effective, including the following:

1. The judge needs to make a finding that alienation dynamics are involved, not that behaviors occurred because it was necessary to protect a child.

2. There will be an investigation into how the behaviors have visibly impacted the child and whether this is a mild, moderate, or severe case of alienation.
3. Based on the severity, the court must determine appropriate remedies:
    a. If it's mild, perhaps psycho-educational programs like co-parenting coaching, counseling, or family systems therapy may work.
    b. When a child has been severely affected, and the other parent's behaviors continue to undermine, sometimes people ask for an immediate change in custody. This can be tricky because of the child's alignment, so steps need to be taken to first improve their relationship with the target parent.

## Connecting the Dots for a Judge

There are all kinds of things you can ask the court for without even mentioning the term parental alienation. If your parenting time has been unilaterally taken away by your ex, Dr. Baker suggests that one option might be filing a motion as a *pro se* (self-represented litigant), documenting that your kid hasn't talked to you in however many weeks/months, and asking for reunification therapy.

Baker says to note to the court that you do not want the child to be forced to come back to your home, but that you are only asking for an hour a week in a therapist's office to make things better. There's no need to explain to the judge how things fell apart, only to say that they aren't in a good place and you'd like therapy, because judges generally support the idea of therapy when kids are struggling.

We're not talking here about reunification camps, a type of immersion treatment which involves multi-day programs with usually three months of aftercare. Alarmists attempting to discredit the entire concept of parental alienation tell scary stories of goons in ski masks pulling children from happy homes in the middle of the night, throwing them in an unmarked van, and forcing them to reunite with their abuser in some mysterious location off the grid. While we have seen those posts, too, we have never seen firsthand a single instance of anything like this in our work, and this is not what we mean by reunification therapy.

Another thing you can do on your own is to file a motion asking for a forensic or custody evaluation rather than putting together a whole case yourself. Why not get a professional to look at what's going on and make some recommendations? Normally, it would take months to prepare for trial, and in the end, all you might get would be reunification therapy anyway, so why not try and get it for free?

Even though this might not be the ultimate goal, it's a first step, especially if you don't have a lot of money and only ask for one hour a week. There is nothing to lose if you have nothing now.

### Habeas Corpus

Attorney Arique Dross says that you can also file a *habeas corpus* petition if you're supposed to have access time and your ex is violating the parenting schedule. This emergency petition asks the judge to order that they physically bring your child to court. If they don't show up, the judge can issue an arrest warrant. Bear in mind that to file something like this requires that you first have a valid court order stating who has custody and when visits are supposed to occur.

Before filing anything, make sure to reach out to your ex in writing. If they don't answer or explicitly state that they're not bringing your child back, this might be appropriate.

## Therapy Clauses in Parenting Plans

In our work with clients, one of the top points of contention is getting mental health services for kids during or after a separation or divorce. But how much time, money, and energy are you willing to spend to get therapy court-ordered?

Divorce attorney Yoni Levoritz says that if therapy for your child isn't already established in your parenting plan, you're likely facing a battle with your ex to get it, so try to have it in your plan from the beginning, even before any court action starts, if possible. In his experience, Levoritz has found courts more likely to order therapy for kids ages six to ten, but less so for older or younger children. Tweens and teens are much harder to drag into therapy if they don't want to go, and preschoolers are so young that judges might not see it as a good solution, even though we know how important it is for children to express themselves - at any age - when they're in a traumatic situation.

If you can't get language explicitly specifying that the child will get therapy, another idea that might be an easier point to negotiate, that is practically the same thing, is to allow therapy if either parent wants the child to have it.

## Damage Control

> "If you just deal with the rejected parent and child, you're not dealing with a lot of the source of the problem."
>
> —Bill Eddy, LCSW, Esq.

Family dynamics are very complex. Choose professionals with proper training who focus on teaching everyone skills, or else they can cause real damage.

According to Bill Eddy, when choosing a counselor for reconciliation between you and your child, the goal should be to teach your child skills for resilience and conflict resolution. This sets the stage for making healthy relationship choices throughout their entire lives, on top of mending your relationship. Eddy notes that for the past several decades, there have been two models for counseling when dealing with parental conflict, but unfortunately, neither fits these nuanced cases.

The first is called the *getting over it* model, which seeks to help everyone move past the divorce and get back to a supposed normal. In our world, things were never *normal*. Simply going back to how things were is unlikely to solve the problem long-term.

The second is the *abuse* model, which pushes victimized children to gradually resume contact until the child feels "safe" again with a parent who has perhaps committed heinous forms of abuse. The difference between these cases and those where a parent has been alienated is significant because that parent had not been abusive.

*Parent-child interaction therapy* (PCIT) focuses on interactions between parent and child together, rather than separate individual therapy, and on skills, rather than past behavior and feelings. This type of therapy has been demonstrably effective in alienation cases.

According to Eddy and other therapists we have spoken with, the best is *family systems therapy*, where the therapist works closely with both parents to strengthen the entire family unit. The structure of the "family" has changed, but it's still a "family unit" from the child's perspective, and the client is really your child. This can be more effective than individual counseling for children, who may still be under the powerful influence of your ex.

Eddy stresses that in all his years of working with professionals involved in family court, "not a single case was resolved by an individual children's counselor unless they worked with the family as well."

### Case Management

To get a court order dictating that therapy must begin often falls by the wayside when there is no follow-up plan already put in place with enforcement language and consequences. Cases like these cannot just be allowed to drift. There are a variety of therapeutic programs with a resolution-focused approach, but strict structure and goals are necessary, as well as monitoring by mental health professionals to ensure that everyone is doing what they're supposed to and progress is being made. Case management might be translated into something called a review hearing or status conference. Usually, a few months after an order has been made or an agreement reached, both parents are expected to return to court so that everyone can ensure that things are moving in the right direction.

The following are questions that Bill Eddy suggests come up frequently, so make sure that you have been doing everything you're supposed to, and you can answer in an honest way that makes the judge and the other court professionals involved happy.

1. Has the child been seeing each parent?
2. Is court-ordered parenting time being scrupulously followed?

3. Have there been any violations? If so, was there makeup time?
4. Was the parent who was ordered not to interfere abiding, or have they continued to violate?
5. If so, is there a plan for contempt, and are sanctions being issued?

Even if a judge finds that alienation has been present, there must be a follow-up. This is the kind of attention needed for situations like yours to get better.

Case management is a follow-up to court orders and ensures that other eyes are on your case besides yours. It's especially helpful to prevent you from having to return to court to keep asking for enforcement. Some jurisdictions have one judge per case who will manage it, set deadlines, and, as Eddy says, "get familiar with who's behaving, who's not… and what needs to be done." Having one judge stick with you allows for a much deeper familiarity with your family and the other players in your case, and prevents having to spend inordinate amounts of time, money, and energy to keep catching up when new judges come on.

At the beginning, it's important to have counseling for everyone if possible. Often, courts order some kind of parenting classes, which are aimed at teaching people skills in moving through divorce and parenting in a healthy way. With case management, dates can be put in place, either six months or a year down the road, when parents can have the opportunity to demonstrate that certain skills have been learned. Case management motivates parents. Everybody wants to show the court they're the better parent, but what's telling is for a judge to start seeing who actually *is* the responsible one.

## Questions for Reflection

1. What specific relief or remedies would be most helpful in your situation (makeup time, custody changes, therapy requirements, etc.)?

2. If you were to file for reunification therapy or an evaluation tomorrow, what would be your strongest argument for why this intervention is needed? What documentation could you use to support this request?

## CHAPTER 12

# WHAT'S MOST IMPORTANT: CREATING STABILITY FOR YOUR KIDS

*"You just don't deserve to live with this level of frustration or pain or anguish, so let's fix it."*

—Mike Barsamian, Parenting Coach

### The Impact of Your Past

If you had an aloof mother or father, you may have grown up believing that love is conditional. You also may have learned how to adjust your behavior to ensure that the parent would take care of you, keep you safe, or even just stick around. This people-pleasing carries into adulthood and becomes your modus operandi, making you a target for an unhealthy relationship dynamic.

Fast forward to now, as you're dealing with your own child's rejection. It feels familiar. And it hurts. So you do what's natural: people-please your kids, says alienation coach Charlie McCready. Even though you are an adult, you may still be afraid of doing the wrong thing and having your child reject you further.

## Triggers and Blockers

McCready believes that our vulnerabilities and insecurities manifest into three things: triggers, blockers, and expectations.

- **Triggers** connect to your sense of self-worth and often tie back to childhood experiences. For example, your child's aggression towards you might make you angry if you were bullied as a child.
- **Blockers** are emotional obstructions that get in the way of accepting the reality of a situation. Obviously, you don't want your child to be experiencing what they are right now, but unfortunately, that is their reality, which you can't change to some extent. But the longer you stay stuck in not accepting things as they are, the more stress it will cause.
- **Expectations** are ideas we create in our heads. No one can help imagining what your kids are going to be like when they're teens, and during milestones like graduations, proms, going off to college, or even way into the future, when there are grandchildren. We fantasize about the first decades of their lives as well as our own role in these fantasies.

What happens is that what we expected and what is happening now are no longer in sync, and this is what causes so much pain. The trick is learning how to realign and reframe our expectations. Finding ways to accept the reality of where we're at doesn't mean giving up hope, but adjusting our perspective, says McCready. It's saying that, as of today, this is what it is.

And therein lies all of the work we have to do. It's a lot. If we are a mess, we won't be able to help our children. To be effective, we have to be in a healed state and learn to create distance from the hurt we might have experienced, so that we can learn to focus our attention not on ourselves, but on our children. They are not obligated to make up for what we did not receive from our own parents.

## Nine On the Emotional Roller Coaster

Charlie McCready says that in the early stages of alienation, things tend to be particularly raw, and we experience nine significant emotions:

1. **Grief.** This "living bereavement" comes in waves; it is over the time you lose today, the time you have already lost, and the time you imagine losing tomorrow.
2. **Guilt.** We are very good at beating ourselves up. It's important to know that this is not your fault.
3. **Shame.** Women tend to face a lot more judgment, and shame tends to affect them more deeply. What kind of a child would leave their mother to go live with their dad?
4. **Isolation.** Bear in mind that most people cannot fathom what you are going through, including those involved with the family court system. More than twenty million people in America alone—including 30% of divorced parents—are experiencing rejection from a child, but rarely do they talk about it.
5. **Powerlessness.** Doesn't it feel like whatever you do is used against you? McCready notes how, if you buy your kid a birthday present, your ex might say that it's a bribe, but if you don't, they'll say that you've forgotten them. Whatever you do or don't do will always be painted in a negative light.

6. **Injustice.** How could this happen, your own child turning against you? And why is nobody helping make it stop?
7. **Anger.** The rage can eat you alive. How could your ex stoop so low?
8. **Anxiety.** We awfulize, imagining all kinds of scenarios where there are dire consequences when what's happening to the kids doesn't stop.
9. **Fear.** The conversation in our head begins with the voice of our ex, and then keeps looping around, especially in moments when we're trying to rest. This fear continues to stoke our anxiety.

These emotions can make it hard to focus on anything.

## Ditching Your Expectations

"Expectations get us into trouble all over the place. The lower your expectations are, the happier you're going to be."

—Susie Pettit, Mental Health Coach

Mental wellness coach Susie Pettit stresses that children actually learn valuable skills from dealing with difficult parental dynamics. This means that we should focus on empowering our children to manage these relationships, rather than attempting to rectify them.

A parent's role is to help their children develop coping mechanisms. Pettit firmly believes that kids have the parents they need to develop into who they are meant to be. She finds acceptance in imagining that her kids have her ex as a parent for a reason: to help them transform into the most amazing woman or man they're going to become. So try as hard as you can to know that you've done everything in your power, take a step back, and trust that this experience might have a greater purpose.

## Retraining and Rewiring

Rebuilding relationships requires trust; you want your kid to feel as stress-free as possible when they come back to you. If they mention activities they're doing with your ex on a weekend that's supposed to be your time, you know you're going to get triggered. You're going to have to work hard on not being reactive and making sure your kid doesn't see how upset you are. This is where the work needs to be done.

Custody evaluator Dr. Mark Singer says that we may unconsciously feed the alienation with comments that end up pushing our kids away. When your child comes back from seeing your ex and says something like, "Mommy thinks you're a piece of sh**," Don't get defensive. Instead, try to deflect. You can say something like, "I understand, but I love you, and let's go outside and throw a baseball or get an ice cream," or whatever you want to do. Patience is key. You have little, if any, control over what your ex is doing. What you *can* control is your own interaction with the kids.

## When They Come Back

Keeping the home chaos-free when they first get back is essential for a peaceful transition. Your children need to know that if they want, they can go upstairs and slam a door or throw something across the room, and they're not going to be punished for it. You're going to send the message that you're here for them to talk, but acknowledge that they need time, and then just wait it out until they're ready. Your kid's nervous system has probably been on overload while they were with your ex, so anything that can slow it down is helpful. This might not be the best time to dive into chores or homework!

When our body is moving, our brain can focus on sensations rather than getting stuck in our heads. Child development specialist AJ Gajjar suggests that on transition days, before even getting back home, take a walk together with the kids. Walking is a form of bilateral movement, which naturally eases stress, and many therapists have noted its benefits, especially with anxious children. It often minimizes emotional dysregulation, as well as provides a connection to nature. Mindful movement instructor Leslie Miller says that kids need to decompress when they return to you, so don't ask questions and let them play with pets if you have them.

We must learn to shield ourselves from anything that distracts us from being present for the kids, including protection from our ex's hate messages. It's hard not to always feel the need to respond, because *if I don't, what if they say something bad, and then what if I don't respond and they tell the judge, and then what if the judge believes something that's not true?* Sound familiar?

All of us deserve downtime. You have a right to peaceful moments with your children, whether it's a weekend or a vacation, without worrying how your ex is going to spin it.

## Dealing With a Sense of Helplessness

But what if they don't come back, and it feels like you're losing them? How do you cope with a child's rejection?

You are going to be in your relationship with your child for a very long time. This means there are going to be opportunities to heal, change, and grow. Remember the past and how close you were, and realize that it can be this way again. Creating a longer, big picture idea of the relationship that's possible is going to help you realize that right now is just temporary.

Founder of Calm Mama Coaching, Darlynn Childress, says we have to figure out what we need in these moments because the one thing we can't do is bring this pain into our relationship with our children. We don't want them to feel like *we* need anything from them.

Childress encourages imagining your child in their twenties, when they're free from the physical parental bonds of your ex, and can learn to create healthy, safe relationships. Imagine yourself calling each other, having meals together, and doing things you dream of doing. Keep holding onto these visions, and trust the likely potential that your kid will come back. And when they do, it might even feel like nothing ever happened.

We have personally experienced and witnessed the restoration of loving relationships after a break. It really does happen more than you could imagine.

## In the Meantime: Dealing with Others When Your Kid Isn't Talking to You

Social events can be extremely stressful when it comes to dealing with other people. One of our clients had completely stopped going to group activities and cried as her old high school friends shared what their families were celebrating during spring break over a group text. How can you not feel excluded?

The senior year of high school is particularly difficult for parents whose children have lost touch. Several of our clients have wept over missing their child's prom or graduation, and feel completely left out of college decisions; some have no idea where their kid has even chosen to go.

Innocent questions from others like "What are your kids up to?" or "How are you going to spend Christmas?" can create a sense of dread. Psychologist Dr. Josh Coleman, author of *Rules of Estrangement*, suggests that if it's someone that you're not close to, say something like, "I don't see him as often as I'd like; he's off in his own world these days," or just mention something you remember from the last time you heard from your child.

Your main goal is to get out of the conversation topic. If you're confronted with stories about other people's children, Coleman suggests saying something complimentary and then excusing yourself to the bathroom.

If an event is going to involve families and their children, and it's going to be too painful, you're allowed to not go and avoid being subjected to what Coleman calls "endless commercials about other people's happy families."

If you absolutely can't get out of it, he recommends writing a script for yourself that contains what you'll say when they show you pictures of their children and ask about yours. You should also map out a clear exit plan, just in case, which can include letting people know ahead of time that you have to leave early for something else.

It's common to become socially withdrawn and feel like you don't want to make others uncomfortable by being sad all the time or requiring so much support. But to friends, talking about what's going on should be similar to discussing any other chronically difficult problem, such as an illness. A close friend will hopefully know that you need to talk about what you're going through, but be conscious that anyone can get burned out.

## My Friends and Family Don't Get It!

Loved ones have a hard time seeing you suffer. We are very familiar with the well-intentioned, "Well, why don't you just…?" When dealing with people close to you who don't seem to get it, try some of the following responses. They might work!

- "I need to be reassured that it's okay to talk about this, at least for now."

- "I know you probably don't mean to, but sometimes you make it seem like this is all my fault."
- "Unfortunately, this is complicated and there's really no easy fix. Please try to understand how difficult this is for me."
- "I just need to feel like someone understands what a nightmare this is. If you could just empathize, that would really help."

Although not everyone will be capable of supporting you, it's certainly worth being clear about what's not helpful and what you need during this time.

## You Can't Get Through This Alone

Children who have been alienated have a lot of power over us. They affect who we are, and this has the potential to make us feel unworthy as a parent and as a person, which is exactly how your ex wants you to feel.

It can seem paralyzing right now, as though there's nothing you can do. Connecting with a community of others can help you remember the good things about yourself and validate who you are, other than just a parent wrangling with a kid who has turned away. Although we may love our children more than anything, they should not be what Josh Coleman calls "the ultimate arbiter of our value."

## Grab Your Cape

Gear up! You've got a lot in front of you, but you can handle it all like you would if you had to eat an elephant: one forkful at a time. You may not realize it yet, but you have superpowers! Your ex targeted you because of how special you are; their association with you made their star shine brighter. It's time to put that specialness to good use in giving your children the kind of environment that will help combat your ex's alienation. To do that, you're going to need to be at your very best, and understanding some of the psychological things you might be dealing with will help.

Parents of kids who have rejected them have to become what Charlie McCready calls "super-parents." You not only have to get through your own issues and healing, but you're also responsible for holding it together for so many others around you: the kids, your new partner, family, friends, as well as yourself. By going through this process, McCready says, you will learn to love at a whole new level.

In normal families, loving your kids is easy. Of course, they can be difficult, but at least they're available. Dealing with a kid who's actively rejecting you forces you to learn to be compassionate, to look through their bad behavior, and instead see that what they are really doing is trying to keep themselves safe.

## Show Yourself Some Grace

If you have a history of being bullied or rejected by your own family as a child, you probably experience more guilt than others and may feel your child's rejection more than most.

There is a gender difference among people whose children have been turned against them that may be connected to societal standards. Men tend to hide their depression with anger and are more likely to withdraw from relationships. Women generally blame themselves more because society expects mothers to revolve their lives around others, especially their own children; if you don't, you're often considered selfish or irresponsible.

The irony, according to Dr. Coleman, is that the skills that made you a good parent are now working against you, because it's more difficult for you to *feel compassion for yourself.* And now is when you need it most.

Try writing out some version of the following, and carry this list around as a reminder to give yourself some grace:

- Since [insert child's name] is choosing to spend time without me, it is healthy to start thinking about how I want to spend my time without them in my life.
- Putting them out of my mind may help me find peace.
- I'm still a good person and a good parent, even if I am not focused on them.
- When I punish myself for the past, I perpetuate the myth that I deserve to suffer. I have suffered enough.
- Today, I will make an effort to feel better about myself as a person and as a parent.

## Peak Condition

Whatever your personal story, we're nearly certain that trauma, at least from your relationship with your ex, is part of it. Please do your best to address whatever would keep you from being in the best shape possible, because combating alienation will ask a lot of you.

Once you have your own proverbial house in order, you can give your full attention to working with your kids, and that's what we get into next.

## Questions for Reflection

1. Looking at Charlie McCready's nine emotions (grief, guilt, shame, isolation, powerlessness, injustice, anger, anxiety, fear), which three affect you most strongly right now?

2. How might these emotions be influencing your interactions with your child?
3. What expectations about your relationship with your child or family life do you think need to be "realigned and reframed" to match your current reality?
4. What specific rituals or routines can you establish (or re-establish) during your time with your child? Think about simple, consistent activities that create good memories. Is there something you can do this week to begin a positive tradition?

## CHAPTER 13

# UNDERSTANDING WHAT'S GOING ON INSIDE THEM: INTERACTING WITH YOUR CHILDREN

*"Instead of asking yourself, 'What could I have done differently?', how about asking, 'What can I do differently moving forward?' "*

— *Tosha Schore,*
*Founder of Parenting Boys Peacefully*

**Why Can't My Kid Just See the Truth?**

We want our kids to recognize that we're the good guy, and their other parent is manipulative. Why can't they just see it?

Pause for a moment. When you were in your abusive relationship, were *you* able to see what was going on? Even as an adult, how long did it take *you* to realize that reality had become warped, and that you couldn't trust the person you loved?

You are playing the long game. The tide may turn in your favor, but trying to force harsh reality onto your child runs the risk of pushing them away. When they attack you based on lies your ex has told them, it's natural to want to set the record straight and convince them exactly how they've been misled. But being overly candid can make your child feel as though you are merely bashing their other parent, and instead of believing you, they may instinctively defend them.

You are also not honoring your kid's ability to draw conclusions for themselves by attempting to define their reality, the same thing your ex is doing. Do not fool yourself that it's more convincing because it happens to be true or comes from you. Instead, you are insulting their intelligence, especially if they are tweens or teenagers, who then think, "Who are you to tell me what to believe?! I can figure it out for myself!"

**Safe Harbor**

Parents are one of the most significant influences on how children understand their world. According to pediatric occupational therapist, Nicole Kristal, *co-regulation* is the "warm, responsive interaction between kids and caregivers (especially us) which models and supports how they can process and understand their thoughts, feelings, and behaviors, which helps them adjust accordingly." To be able to provide this, we need to self-regulate, to keep ourselves in check, and manage our thoughts and feelings so that we can focus on goal-directed behaviors. This is a necessary foundation for co-regulation with our children.

When our child reports something vicious our ex has said, we may be triggered and feel that past abuse all over again, making us fear that the kids believe our ex, or worse, that they are turning into little narcissists themselves. It's natural to feel inflamed, but kids need us to be as calm as possible. We therefore need to acknowledge our triggers and figure out ways to calm ourselves down in the moment, so that we can respond to our kids with compassion. Don't worry if you've already lost your cool in front of your kids, no matter how badly, recently, or often. None of us is perfect. You can't do anything about the past, and every single day is a fresh opportunity to improve. Here are three ways to start making yourself a source of comfort again:

1. **Make sure that your kids see that you are not giving any credence to lies or even getting upset about them.** This shows them that you are confident in the truth and not afraid of false accusations.
2. **Have predictable routines.** This is how kids develop a sense of security.
3. **Model how to respond in a variety of scenarios**, which we are getting into throughout this chapter.

## The Long Game

Remember back to your child's first days when you wondered what to do with this tiny baby? When babies are born, the pediatrician gives parents little books that say what to expect developmentally each month. Most of us, unfortunately, stop keeping track after the first year.

Why don't we continue to pay attention to our middle and high schoolers? We still need to keep an eye on what they're saying and doing, and take note. Are their eating patterns changing? What about sleep?

These observations should not be saved for annual checkups. Instead, they might open the door to having a conversation.

## Meet Them Where They're At

Josh Coleman urges you to "live in their world for a while before asking them to take a step into yours." As tragic as it is, this is the way they see things for now. Telling them that they're wrong will just upset them further, making them more likely to shut down. Instead of pointing out how distorted your child's thoughts are, try using language that acknowledges what they're feeling (e.g., anger), shows that you can see why they feel that way, and that if it were you, you'd probably feel the same. Doing this may allow them to let down their guard. By not defending yourself at the moment, you are actually "strengthening your authority," says Coleman, because of your willingness to see things from their point of view, and demonstrating an ability for self-examination (a wonderful thing to model).

### Two Magic Lines

You've got to find a way to have open communication with your kid, and for them to know that when they are talking, you are listening. You have what former lawyer turned empowerment coach Nicolle Kopping-Pavars calls responsibility, meaning specifically a *"response ability,"* and you can learn to respond appropriately. According to the founder of ParenT(w)een Connection, Clarissa Constantine, the following two phrases are virtually guaranteed to elevate you in your child's eyes:

- "Hey, I appreciate your insight."
- "Thank you. I will work on that."

These statements are disarming and show that what your kid says matters. When you value their input, they will gain a sense of being part of something bigger than themselves as they participate in creating solutions.

### Turn "Why?" Into "What?"

Asking open-ended questions that show you care helps defuse and disarm. Even if your kids brush you off initially or tell you to leave them alone, if you are consistent, they're going to connect. Parenting coach Mike Barsamian works hard at never asking "why?" because, although it's a valid question, it can be a trigger. Instead, every *why* question can be turned into a *what*. Behavioral analyst Theresa Inman also stopped asking "why?" because she noticed that it feels judgmental and causes people to put up their guard. "What" questions allow an opportunity to connect. If your kid is upset, find out *what* happened. Instead of asking, "Are you ok?" (which just gets an automatic "yes"), try, "What can I do to help you?"

## Teaching Emotional Literacy

Recognizing and decoding how others feel is empathy. And to have empathy for others, claims parenting coach Darlynn Childress, a person must first master emotional literacy; it's as important as learning the alphabet.

To be emotionally literate requires knowing:

- What I'm feeling
- How to vocalize that feeling
- What to do with it

Childress believes that when children are experiencing big feelings, they need support because they don't always understand why they're acting the way they are. One strategy she encourages parents to use when communicating with kids is the phrase, "I wonder if..." and then to guess what they might be feeling. It's more open-ended than a statement such as, "I know you're feeling \_\_\_\_," which instead claims that you understand how they feel and can seem judgmental. A lot of times, our child may experience several feelings mixed together, which can be hard to explain.

"You gotta name it to tame it," says Mike Barsamian. Many kids only know three basic emotions: happy, angry, and sad. But there's also a complex set of secondary and tertiary emotions, and when we can identify those, we have more control over them. Emotional regulation helps our kids see those emotions more clearly and hold their hands throughout.

Another common mistake parents make is asking a child, "What are you feeling?" This is so open-ended that it can feel overwhelming, especially to someone who may lack the vocabulary to articulate exactly what they feel at that moment. You want to narrow it down, like turning an essay question into true or false. Say instead something like, "Are you nervous?" because then it's an easier yes or no, and hopefully starts getting to the root of what's going on inside.

## Easing the Stress of Transitions

Think about when you come back from a trip, how it takes a day or two to get back into your work mindset. Bear in mind that children of divorce often go through this every week. Barsamian says that one of the easiest ways to create peace at home is to have a receiving routine where you give your kids some time to readjust. Be welcoming, hospitable, and open, knowing that they need some space to get resettled. For kids dealing with separate homes, inconsistency is a permanent way of life, notes psychologist, author, and professor Dr. Christopher Willard. *Did I remember to bring my homework back from Mom's house? I miss my friend at Dad's.*

Our kids have to *code-switch* as they go between two homes and figure out how to operate with two parents whose mindsets may be very different. They are essentially living in two different cultures, as each parent runs their home a certain way, so of course, we should expect an adjustment period when they come back. Dr. Willard suggests having some of their favorite snacks and something they can snuggle with, if it's age-appropriate, allowing them to reset.

The teenage years are like walking a tightrope, says Barsamian, with all kinds of uncertainty. They've got one pole in the ground in childhood and the other in adulthood, and it can be hard to find balance as their minds are shifting, changing, and developing.

Unscheduled downtime allows kids' brains to get back into a place where they can start functioning at a high level again. Often, teenagers like to retreat to their rooms for a while. Give them some space to decompress and return to being with you. You can let them know that you're there if and when they need you.

## Understanding Dysregulated Kids

Child developmental specialist AJ Gajjar says that our kids are often "living in a stress response, surviving a traumatic environment" while at our ex's house. These feelings do not immediately go away when they come back to us. Getting them out of it means it's on us to provide and recreate a sense of safety through predictability and consistency.

When you already know that the kids are going to be dysregulated, make transition day as low-key as possible. Let your child have more options. Maybe allow them to choose what's for dinner that night. Some kids find comfort in an area to retreat to, such as a tent. Others love sound machines, twinkly lights, cozy, fluffy blankets, or pillows. One of our client's daughters would go into the bathroom, lie her head on the sink, and stare at the running water for a few minutes. Creating a quiet sensory place is a great idea. There are a number of ways you and your kid can turn this space into an activity to do together, even without spending a lot of money. It's really about getting attuned to your child's needs.

## My Kid is Turning Into My Ex!

It's hard to feel compassion for children who are mimicking the same toxic behavior as your ex. After all, did you go through all it took to get away, only to end up with another younger version? As hard as it is, try not to take the things your kid says and does personally. Your child is exactly that: a child. They are malleable, and your ex is an influential presence in their life in addition to being a highly skilled manipulator who has, in all likelihood, been honing his or her skills since adolescence. We might forget that our children are experiencing *cognitive dissonance,* meaning that their thoughts, feelings, and beliefs are inconsistent with their perceptions, because they are being exposed to conflicting messages. This is what makes processing all that's going on so difficult. In many ways, our kids are living the same experience we did, but with *less* emotional maturity to process it.

## The Importance of Rituals

Don't we all love things to look forward to? Wellness coach Kristen Darcy agrees on the importance of having rituals for when your kids transition back to your home. She would often have Trader Joe's fresh flowers waiting in her daughter's bedroom to welcome her back. She also did something we highly recommend called *indirect journaling* with her kids, where she used a composition notebook to write a journal entry to them when they were away, so that when they came back, there was a little note waiting. There was never any pressure or expectation for them to write back to her. Over the years, they created memory books, tangible evidence of a deep, intimate connection.

Making plans with our kids to do fun things together, whether it's something short-term like a picnic, concert, visiting friends, cooking a favorite dish, or longer-term, like a vacation, can help boost everyone's mood. This is what "helps us stay connected around the positive," says Dr. Christopher Willard. Our kids need good memories.

Even in the tornado of all the fighting, kids who have rituals will remember them fondly, like hot chocolate nights every Thursday, or trips to Cape Cod every summer for a week with their cousins. Put things on a calendar that you can all look forward to. Invite your kid to participate because this allows them to feel like they have some control. Planning activities together, even meals, creates moments that you can take time to talk with them about. Making sure children have positive memories during their childhood will help them connect with themselves when they get older.

## But I'm Still Angry

Psychologist Dr. Alina Boie notes how kids can get confused when they see you're upset. Don't pretend that everything is fine; instead, acknowledge those uncomfortable feelings. Say something like, "I feel kind of down today. It's been very hard, but you know what? I'm going to see what I can do to feel better. What do you suggest? What do you do when you feel sad or disappointed?" Even a three-year-old can help contribute, notes Boie, which makes them feel good. You are teaching them how to care for someone who's upset, and that even I, a grown-up, can ask for help!

By basically swapping roles, you are giving your child a chance to coach you, which a lot of kids love. You're also displaying your humanity, the fact that you have ups and downs, and that it's okay to admit that something's wrong. It's okay not to be perfect. And it can be heartwarming when you see your child try to solve a problem along with you and come up with a creative solution, such as:

> "Hey Mom, I think you should just put your pajamas on, make some popcorn with the cheese powder, and go watch *Bridesmaids*, since that always makes you laugh, and I know you'll feel better!"

You are also teaching empathy without pulling them into the details of your chaos by focusing on the feeling, such as frustration, while modeling how to cope with it, rather than trying to fix something that may be unfixable right now.

## Pace Parenting

You may be making lunches, helping them get dressed, and teaching them to tie their shoes, but when you get to the teen years, it's about "trust development," says Mike Barsamian. And trust is about self-confidence, accountability, standards, boundaries, and expectations, which are not synonymous. He compares this stage of parenting to running a marathon, where you're trying to get your kid across the finish line to adulthood, but you don't get to do it from the sidelines. Instead, you must run the race with them, like "pacemakers," athletes who run with a mile sign displaying the pace at which they are running. They train just as hard, get dehydrated, and hurt their hips, knees, and feet just as much. And although they too have to cross the finish line, they don't get a medal because it's not their race. Their goal is to encourage and cheer you on. They are there so you win, but they experience all the same pain because they're running just as hard.

As parents, he says, the first thing to do is just put some pads on and get a helmet because it's live training. You've helped your kids get to the starting line of their adult years, and you've still got to run with them, but remember, *it's not your race.*

## Questions for Reflection

1. Think of a recent conflict you had with your child. Do you think your child was trying to approach you, to make a connection, ask for help, or try to express uncomfortable feelings?
2. How did you react or respond?
3. How did the way you dealt with it affect your child?
4. How did you feel about the way you handled it? What, if anything, worked well?
5. What, if anything, would you do differently?

## CHAPTER 14

# WHEN ANGER BECOMES AGGRESSION

*"The path out of hell is through misery."*

— *Marsha Linehan,*
*Founder of Dialectical Behavior Therapy*

### Dealing With a Child's Rage

Imagine having your own kid break your nose, or scream in front of a group of their friends' parents how much they "hate you."

Our clients have experienced this, and far worse. They've confessed to being physically attacked and emotionally destroyed by their own children. One woman told us how her son, in a fit of rage, poured olive oil all over the couch and floors, then cut off his hair and scattered chunks of it amongst the mess. That takes destruction to impressive new levels.

Shame can make you silent: first, because you're blaming yourself, second, because your ex is claiming that this never happens with them, and lastly, because something deep inside you may also be whispering that you deserve this.

## Is This Normal?

Your kids are affected the most by your split. They can't just walk away, because they are still dependent, usually on both of you. It's natural for them to want to blame someone for the chaos. The foundation of their whole life—the family unit—has been ripped apart, and now they are torn between two parents who appear to be mortal enemies. They're probably struggling just to get through each day.

Every piece of advice given to a parent going through this major life change is to send kids the message that it's not their fault, that the problems are strictly between two grown-ups, and that you will both always love and put them first. So why do they lash out at you and not your ex?

Bear in mind that your ex is intentionally twisting the narrative, making you the villain. The divorce is your fault. You are the one abandoning the family or committing a sin. Only they will continue to love and keep your kids safe. Instead of working with you cooperatively, your ex may intentionally exacerbate problems and then reward your child for turning away from you. Thus, your kid's rage often lands on you.

According to child development specialist AJ Gajjar, the protective, loving parent often gets the brunt of explosive feelings and meltdowns because the child knows on some level that you're the safe parent and they trust that you're not going anywhere. This may make sense, but it doesn't make it easy.

## Sometimes They Don't Know Better

Behavioral analyst Theresa Inman often says, "How many times have I heard a parent tell a two-year-old, 'You know better than this!' And I'm thinking, they don't. They are merely mirroring what they see in the environment." From birth to age seven, children are in a *meditative state*, not making conscious decisions, but simply reacting to what they've seen and experienced. We have to be mindful of what we expose our children to, whether it be what they watch on television, the games that they play, or our behavior. What are we modeling?

## Try Not to Say "Boundaries"

The word boundaries is overused. When you tell an angry kid that you need to set a boundary with them, it can feel demeaning, as though you're saying, "You are so awful that I need to make special rules just for you." Sometimes, just the utterance of the word makes it sound like you don't want them around.

Dr. Amy Baker suggests that a more constructive solution is to use phrases that send positive messages, such as, *This is how I hope things will be between us*. It's the difference between "Don't spill your milk!" and "Hold your cup a little tighter."

## Why Can't I Defend Myself?

The last thing you want is to put your kid back on the battlefield. That's exactly what we inadvertently do when we defend ourselves against our ex's narrative to our children. You're actually estranging yourself even more from your child because you're putting the kids under additional pressure. Remember, they are afraid of your ex. They know that if they don't defend and keep that other parent happy, they will be punished or, worse, cast aside.

Alienation coach Charlie McCready says that pushing back and saying their other parent is lying forces your kids into the one conversation they don't want to have: where they need to consider that one of their parents is not telling the truth. And they may already be convinced that you're the liar. When you defend yourself and who you are, you are prioritizing your own need to prove something, showing a lack of respect for your child's ability to draw their conclusions. You're letting them know indirectly that you do not trust their judgment, nor their capacity to discern what's real. You're also moving the spotlight away from the person who matters most here: your child.

Furthermore, if you micromanage, you're depriving them of agency, potentially leading to power struggles. Instead, Clarissa Constantine says it is important to stay quiet for a bit. Once we start talking, it can also be helpful to avoid "you" statements, like "You need to calm down," or "You need to respect me." Focus on how what they're saying or doing makes *you* feel, and instead use "me" statements, like, "It's hard for me to understand you when you talk to me in this tone of voice because it hurts my feelings." The same applies if they are lying to you. Instead of being confrontational, find another way to state that you see things differently. In this way, you're not blaming them, but focusing instead on your own feelings, which are indisputable, and how what your kid is doing is affecting you.

Many kids fantasize that you and your ex will get back together, and they won't have to deal with any of this. When you force them to choose between you, they don't know what to believe, because the two people that they're supposed to trust the most are telling them completely different stories. Some children react to all of this by regressing. They may act several years younger than they are developmentally, and wet their beds or suck their thumbs again. Or they may do something called *splitting*, where they see one parent as good and the other as bad, which is both highly traumatic and difficult to recover from, even as they get older.

### Attacking My Parent Gives Me Power

Kids don't often have much agency, and figuring out how to knock a parent off balance can be, well, entertaining. When we lose control, we may not even realize that we are inadvertently rewarding our children for the very thing we can't stand.

Consider this possibility: might your ex be encouraging your child to get you riled up? Only to later grill them to report back your reaction…to later use against you?

One of our clients was on vacation with her son, and a heated argument turned physical. This had happened before, and her ex grilled their son for a blow-by-blow description. We're sure you can guess what kind of court motions were filed right after they returned home. Think about the high your ex gets from any attention you give them, especially negative. Do we now want to provide a similar hit to our own children?

This is why being measured matters. And we already know it is not easy! By staying as calm as you can, and trying to listen for the *meta*—what's really beneath the words—you won't mistakenly confirm exactly what poisonous message the other parent is trying to send, like: "Dad's right, Mom's crazy" or "Mom's right, Dad's out of control." When we strongly react to the words coming out of our child's mouth, we show them how to inflame us in an instant, and that's powerful.

## Dealing with Disrespect

When blowouts occur on a regular basis, you've got to prepare ahead of time. Here are some things to think about:

1. What are your goals? If there are points you want to make, write two or three of them down.
2. **Practice ahead of time,** saying them out loud, preferably to someone else or a mirror.
3. Just as importantly, have an exit plan. How will you get away if it is unproductive or even confrontational?

4. At the very beginning of an interaction, if not ahead of time, see if there's a way to establish ground rules. You can say something like, "In the past, we've had a hard time communicating, but I really want to hear what you have to say. Is there a way we could both agree to try hard to be as calm as possible?"
5. Express that you recognize that your child has something important to say. Make it clear that you believe they have good intentions and that you appreciate it.
6. Let them go first. Ask them to start with what they're hoping to get out of the conversation. Then it will be your turn. Ask if that works for your kid.
7. Repeat what you believe your child perceives as the problem, even if they feel like you never understand anything.
8. If your child starts losing their temper, describe how difficult it is to want to know what they have to say, but not be able to listen because they are being hostile.
9. Propose a solution to the communication issue. You might want to say something like, "Can we try again, in a calmer tone, so I can focus better on what I know you want me to understand?"
10. Let them know it's okay to express negative emotions, as long as it doesn't come out in an emotionally or physically violent way. You can say something like, "It's ok to be mad, or even say that you hate me, but please don't curse at me or hit me."
11. If the hostility continues, refer to your exit plan. Say something like, "If we can't at least use a respectful tone with each other, I'm going to have to end the conversation now/hang up/leave the room."

12. Follow through. If they continue being disrespectful, end the conversation.
13. Follow up. Within a day, check in on them to see how they're doing, and ask if they would like to try again. If they don't, just say you're here when they're ready.
14. Do it again. Keep trying to have a productive interaction using the same steps.

## Two Fundamental Needs

What do kids and narcissists have in common? They want the same two things: control and attention. We all need to feel like we are part of something, like a family or a community, and to feel significant. According to psychologist Dr. Alina Boie, when a child lacks control and attention, they will not feel that sense of belonging and will do anything to get it. For example, if a parent is never providing positive attention, their child may be more likely to smack a sibling, which would certainly get attention. Good attention or bad attention, both fulfill that same need.

## What's the Purpose?

Your child's behavior serves a purpose, whether it be to relieve stress or attempt to express something. Theresa Inman suggests that we become detectives and document through a diary, answering the following:

- How did you (and your child) say what was said?
- How were you feeling when you said it?
- What were you projecting?
- What in the environment changed before this behavior?

Every behavior has a function. When a child becomes aggressive, we must look at the greater context, especially what happened just beforehand. "That whole chain is what's going to determine if this behavior continues, or if it decreases and extinguishes," says Inman. Bear in mind that when we, as parents, are in a heightened state of stress, our child picks up on that energy and may behave in ways that they don't even understand. It ties back to how we are presenting to them. We can teach them how to express themselves better or differently by how we express ourselves, Inman says.

## Escalation to Physical Violence

Whether your child is acting out physically or not, their behavior is underscored by some feeling of abandonment, and you should approach them with compassion. They are in pain and struggling with emotions they have no skills to deal with (yet). Sometimes kids can ramp up to the point where they are physically violent, whether to you directly or to your home, and common sense should prevail to ensure that everyone is physically safe.

A normal reaction when things get out of control might be to call the police. Custody evaluator Dr. Mark Singer stresses that this should be viewed as a last resort. Your ex will surely take advantage of any opportunity to vilify you by feeding your child a narrative that you called the police because you think they're bad or dangerous. Your child wants you to love them, not be afraid of them. As with any child who is acting explosively, a key is turning your volume down when they turn theirs up. Easier said than done!

## Triage: Three Things You Can Do in the Moment

### Tip One: Give Them Space…for Now!

When tensions are too high to accomplish anything useful, consider physically removing yourself, if possible. Start by announcing what the consequences will be if they don't stop attacking, and make it clear that the choice is theirs. For example, "If you're going to speak to me like that, I'm going to leave the room. I can see how angry you are, and when you calm down, we can talk about it, because I really do want to understand how you feel."

Here you are showing that you care, but at the same time signaling that you will not tolerate inappropriate, abusive behavior. Make sure to follow through because if you don't and continue the argument, you will be rewarding them with your negative attention. Not good. The benefit of doing this well will be a shift in the power dynamic in the relationship with your child. This will not happen quickly, and bear in mind that your kids are not going to be happy about your attempts to start asserting yourself. With practice, things should improve.

And, to the people-pleasers out there: this will be tough! As we've discussed, we all bring emotional baggage to our parenting. Chris in particular struggled with this, having been conditioned from an early age that love is something you need to pursue, coupled with an ex trying to take his kids' hearts away… this can be a challenging one-two punch to overcome!

### Tip Two: Be Inquisitorial

Another technique is to slow things down and turn inquisitorial, meaning to approach the situation with curiosity. We lean on this approach a lot in our work with our clients, and it's a two-step process. First, when your children come at you angrily, try to pause before reacting. This is going to be hard when you first do it! In that pause, observe feelings, both your child's and your own.

Next, remember that your child is suffering. Sometimes it's hard not to see them as an enemy. But they, too, are victims of domestic violence—emotional abuse, at the very least. They're still in a relationship with an abuser. And they're children. They don't have the emotional maturity to process all of it.

And finally, feelings first. Tell yourself that you can tackle a specific concern *only after* your child's feelings have been addressed. This is worth repeating because it's so important: the goal is not the truth, but to deal with your child's feelings, and nothing else…yet.

Parenting coach Darlynn Childress loves using "I wonder…" statements. These are helpful because they sound like you are *trying to* figure things out, rather than dictating to your child how they should see or feel things. For example: "I wonder if you're mad at me because I didn't come to your school play. I could see how it could look like I was so busy that I completely forgot, and that somehow you don't matter to me." Remember, your ex may have tried to portray you as unloving or unavailable to your child, who is already feeling abandoned.

The "I wonder…" approach can be incredibly powerful, especially with younger kids, who may be surprised that you are so in tune with their feelings that you can zero in on what's bothering them and why. You can follow with something like this: "I want you to know that actually, I wasn't included in the email with the details and didn't even know that it was tonight. I'm so sorry, and I feel terrible that I missed it, and want you to know that I love you. Can you tell me about what happened or show me what you did? I will do everything I can to make sure this doesn't happen again."

By offering an explanation for what's upsetting them, you're showing how deeply you care that they feel badly. All of this can be disarming, and fingers crossed, spark a deeper conversation. Never blame your ex for putting ideas in your kid's head! Let them draw their own conclusions. Your goal is to shore up your relationship with your child, not win a battle of loyalties, and right now, you just don't want your child to shut down.

**Tip Three: Demonstrate Your Amazing Empathy**
Let's not become what Canadian therapist and author Marnie Grundman calls "bubble wrap parents" who try to insulate children in every way possible. If your kids are provided an opportunity to process what they are experiencing, they can sharpen critical thinking skills. Try asking, "What do you mean by that? How does that make you feel?"

Try as hard as you can to understand your child's perspective. The best way to protect our children from falling prey to poisonous messages and other alienating behaviors is to continue to build a strong, solid relationship with them, and this takes work on a regular basis. To be proactive, make sure your child has enough positive attention from you. Spending quality time and building rapport with your child is essential, says school psychologist Dr. Boie, who teaches parents how to "glow and grow" together. She suggests doing an activity that your child enjoys, whether you like it or not. The point is to let them take the lead and guide whatever it is you're doing together. If you are in the middle of crazy court stuff, this is an even better opportunity to just pause and not allow your pain into what should be cherished time with your child.

During these few minutes together, give your undivided attention, make sure that you are able to have fun, and hopefully laugh together. For example, you can ask them to show you how to cook something that they make well, even if it's brownies from a box. Lisa used to walk their family dog to school every day with her kids, even when they were angry (on those days they were not walking next to each other!). The important thing was that she was showing up, with actions, not words.

The goal is to connect with your child in a positive way consistently and keep building those good memories that they will keep in their hearts and brains for the rest of their lives. Reliably "showing up" demonstrates that you are a rock who will always be there for your kids, no matter what. Boie says that they will start to bond, trust, and open up differently, and that there's nothing you can do that's more impactful over time than being faithfully present for your child.

## Own Your Volcanoes

North Carolina family therapist and professor Dr. Kristin Roorbach says that one thing you have power over is your own language to your children, which consists of three parts:

1. **Your children can't keep you healthy.** It is your own responsibility to be the adult in the room, which means you need to find a way to be as neutral and loving in your environment as possible. Statements like, "I live for my kids," unfortunately, put a tremendous weight on your child, who then feels responsible on some level for your happiness.
2. Unless you're taking care of yourself and can stay grounded during these encounters, you are not as healthy as you should be. This is going to require support. You're going to have to model loving boundaries and clear messages, and this is not easy under volatile conditions.

3. Know that you're going to overreact and not behave perfectly all the time, possibly within earshot of your kids. Roorbach says "owning your volcano" means saying that you're sorry for that reaction, even though you're not sorry for your feelings because you're going through a lot, and your child is, too. You can acknowledge when you don't do a great job of controlling yourself. You can explain that you need to work on it, that you're going to take a minute to take care of yourself, and voice out loud that it is not their responsibility to take care of you.

Being as open, consistent, and authentic as possible will strengthen the bond between you and your child and help shield against your ex's attempts to sever your relationship.

### Myths of Aggression

Tosha Schore, an expert on aggression in kids and the founder of Parenting Boys Peacefully, says that parents of aggressive boys *and* girls often have several misconceptions, including some of the following:

1. **Putting distance between the two of you is a good idea.** It's natural to want to banish your child, especially when conflict has been ongoing and you're emotionally exhausted. Sending your child away isolates and punishes them for having feelings that don't match yours. Certainly, take a few minutes to calm yourself down, but know that pushing your child away perpetuates the problem.

2. **Believing that you need to "teach" your child that their behavior is bad.** In a heated argument, everyone is running on adrenaline and unable to think straight. It can be

hard to come up with the right things to say, so if you can be quiet, it will allow you to see that your child may be calling for help. Try to listen.

3. **Imagining that listening is not going to solve anything.** In the short term, yes, you are allowing your kids an outlet for their feelings without directly addressing their dysregulation, Schore explains. Having helped hundreds of parents in the same situation, she's learned that in the long term, the aggressive behaviors subside when children have a way to get them out. So try to be as silent and present as you can be.

4. **Thinking that not immediately issuing consequences will embolden your child.** Right now is not the time for punishment. The truth is that your child is doing the best that they can. Do you want them to feel as though you only love them when things are fine, but when things get hard, they are supposed to deal with them alone? Schore asserts that sending the message that you will be there to get through things with them together is much more effective.

Remember how your ex's love was conditional, a reward for your good—no, perfect—behavior? Your child is experiencing that same dynamic now in their relationship with your ex.

## The Thirty Second Rule

You want your kid to develop the ability to contemplate complex issues before forming opinions, and keeping your mouth shut will force them to do so. Clarissa Constantine challenges us to give our children thirty seconds to think when asking more than a simple yes/no question. Take yourself out of their immediate presence if you can't muzzle yourself! Otherwise, do whatever it takes to give them the space and time to respond, which means you can wash dishes, pet the dog, or find a speck on the wall to concentrate on. After you've let half a minute pass, before saying a word, ask yourself, "Am I responding from a place of my own emotional hurt, or am I responding from a place of supporting them in their growth?"

### How to Respond in the Immediate Moment

In the midst of an argument with your kids, it's impossible to make good decisions. High levels of the stress hormone cortisol can provoke feelings of urgency, which can translate into feeling as though everything is an emergency.

When your brain is screaming to respond, force yourself to pause. Your body is feeling the effects of trauma, and it's necessary to try to calm down before reacting this very second with big emotions. We can reset our nervous system through bilateral movement, using both sides of the body in a coordinated manner, including:

- Walking
- Riding a bike
- Washing dishes
- Doing jumping jacks
- Rubbing your hands together
- Tapping

Doing something physical that is rhythmic, using more than one of your senses, such as sight, sound, or touch, can help process trauma and is a great way to calm down after your brain has been hijacked.

## When You Mess Up

Judge Lynn Toler, a former family court judge and star of the TV show *Divorce Court*, has something called the "Up Rule," which is, **"When you mess up, fess up. Back up, then clean up."**

Acknowledging your own mistakes will turn down the volume on your kids' anger. After all, it's hard for anyone (except maybe your ex) to stay furious at someone admitting, "You're completely right. That was totally my fault, and I'm so sorry."

Doubt and self-torment are common after a fight, even when the other person has been abusive. Instead of berating yourself, Psychologist Dr. Josh Coleman recommends the following to get back in alignment:

- **Remind yourself of your good intentions.** You didn't want to fight; you only tried as hard as you could to be closer to your kid.

- **Engage in a self-soothing activity.** Remember that your nervous system was on high alert, and even after an altercation, stress hormones were coursing through your body. It's now time to calm down by doing something to distract yourself, such as exercise, meditation, or one of Lisa's personal favorites, journaling. The act of writing out what happened naturally forces your body to slow down and can help lower stress, as well as provide a record to reflect on later.

- **Forgive yourself.** If you were provoked, try to do better next time.

## Limits

First and foremost, **model being in control of your own emotions** *without trying to control theirs.* Here are more practical tips Coleman suggests:

- **Listen in a non-defensive way to what your child is saying.** No matter how cruel it may be, see if there is some kernel of truth in it, even if it's inconsistent with how you remember things. Try to view this from their perspective, and not as a matter of right or wrong.
- **Explain that you know they have something important to communicate,** and you would like to hear it, but you can't listen when the tone is this hostile.
- **Don't criticize your child for not communicating well;** remember, they are trying. Say something simple like, "That's probably not going to work for me," or "No, I won't do that, but I am willing to _____."
- **Don't let yourself be blackmailed.** Remember, you don't have to answer immediately. You are allowed to say you need some time to think about what they just said.
- **Empathize with what they are feeling or saying.** Teens often feel a tremendous amount of shame. Try, "*I can see why you would feel/think* \_\_\_\_." This is much better than confronting them over something you feel they did wrong.
- **And if you have a chance, ask specifically what they would like from you.** It could be useful ahead of time to think about what you are willing to do, so you don't feel completely pressured by their response. When you've decided, try to separate your decision from your feelings of guilt or intimidation.

Understand that older children, in particular, have a need to save face. Lines like these allow them to do so:

- "Maybe you're right."
- "I can see how things might have been better if we'd done them differently."
- "I'm sorry - I had no idea you felt this way at the time."
- "I now understand how that would have been much better for you."
- "I didn't know that you needed something different from me, and I apologize for missing this."

One way to surprise your child is to ask for help, especially on how to avoid conflict in the future. Is there an agreement you might be able to make where you will each try to bring up something when it's bothering you, rather than letting things build up?

By telling them that you're interested in their communication with you on what you do wrong, you're *building credibility*; you're letting them know that you're *open to working on yourself.*

## Questions for Reflection

1. What generally precipitates a blowout between you and your child? What are two ways you can reset yourself, whether through bilateral movement or some other way?
2. Think about a recent conflict with your child. Looking beneath their words and behavior, what underlying feelings or fears might they have been trying to express?
3. Consider a recurring complaint or accusation from your child. How could you reframe your response using an "I wonder..." statement that demonstrates empathy and

understanding of their perspective, rather than defending yourself or correcting their narrative?

4. What are two things you can do with your child for the "10-minute rule" where they are leading or guiding you through an activity?

CHAPTER 15

# DEALING WITH THE DEVIL

*"After our divorce, my kids were struggling to figure out who was the right parent."*

—Amber Chapman, Writer

**Leverage & Influence**

We've already discussed solutions in the legal system and your own parenting, but how about things you can do through direct communication with your ex? Before you cry, "Hopeless!" and skip to the next chapter, please understand that this is not about rebuilding your co-parenting relationship with your ex to usher in some new era of cooperation. We know that's not going to happen.

However, your unique advantage is that you likely know them better than anyone else does. After all, you probably spent years trying in vain to figure out what was wrong in your relationship and how you could change yourself to make them happy, or at least just to survive. Think about your ex for a moment. What motivates them? What makes them fearful? What vulnerabilities do they have?

Many narcissists are deeply afraid of being exposed: legally, publicly, or to the kids. While some scoff at judges' orders and view themselves as entirely above the law, others are concerned about appearances, including how they're viewed in court. Some want to be seen as a model citizen and fear being exposed in court for their explicit violations of the parenting plan or other malicious behavior. Or they might be a public figure, even a minor one; not "famous," but in some role, professionally or socially, where a public callout would cause them humiliation and pain. Narcissists hate that. That's leverage, too. A lot of times, legal proceedings are a matter of public record.

Leverage can be anything that motivates your ex to reach some kind of agreement that you can live with without having to go through the expense and uncertainty of a trial. Note that that doesn't mean you won't have to file something in the legal system; it means that, whatever the issue is, it doesn't go all the way to a trial. Even high-conflict cases settle most of the time.

People like your ex usually hire the nastiest bullies who enable their nonsense for a payday. However, if you're lucky enough to have reasonable opposing counsel, a highly professional attorney may give your ex a dose of reality, allowing you to avert a protracted, expensive fight ... if your ex will listen.

## They Don't Know You ... Anymore

They studied you when they drew you in, then tore you down; that's the *you* they know. They have no clue that you're rebuilding yourself and getting stronger. They probably won't know how to deal with the *you* that you are becoming. Keep it that way. Don't tell them what you're learning; keep your education a secret weapon, at least for now. This is about solving a problem, and in the case of alienation, a very significant one. It's not about your pride or proving something: letting them feel like they're winning is a strategy.

## Strategic Communication

In our coaching practice, we spend more time on our clients' communication with their exes than on any other single subject area. We help them keep their messages as brief as possible and devoid of any emotion to turn the power dynamic around while building powerful documentation for the court.

A lot of what we help clients write follows our *FRAC Model*, which has four parts:

> **FACT**—something you observed or was reported to you.
>
> **REACTION** — confusion or surprise, never "shock" or "concern" that whatever happened, happened.
>
> **AGREEMENT** —a universal agreement or "anchor" that provides the indisputable standard by which any potential solution or action will be evaluated.
>
> **COLLABORATION** — an invitation for them to work cooperatively with you to address whatever the issue is.

As an example, suppose your ex is not having your child do the video calls with you that are specified in your parenting plan, which translates to blocking contact, a huge no-no. Every communication should be in writing, ideally in a parenting app, and we recommend you send a message like this:

"For the past three weeks, my scheduled calls with the kids have not been happening. (FACT) This is confusing (REACTION), as I'm sure we can both agree on how important it is that we support their having regular contact with each of us. (AGREEMENT/ANCHOR). How can we work together to ensure that no further calls are missed?" (COLLABORATION)

A lot is being accomplished in this relatively simple message. For starters, you're very clearly calling them out for their misbehavior. In the example, your ex is violating the parenting plan, which is a binding legal agreement. As long as their behavior runs counter to the values of the court, and number one on that list is the importance of having two involved parents who support each other's relationship with your child, they would probably not look good to a third party, whether or not you have a court order.

Communicating with your ex this way helps build your case, and if done well, will portray you as a shining star of cooperation in the face of a really difficult co-parent. There is no more consistently compelling evidence in custody disputes than your direct written communication with your ex.

When you send a message like this, you can expect one of three things to happen. First, they might ignore it entirely. In that case, you can follow up after a short time with another message that has "Second request" in the subject line and briefly reminds them of the ongoing problem. Sticking with our example, this next one might say:

"The scheduled calls with the kids have not been happening for six weeks. How can we ensure that this is corrected?"

If they continue to ignore you, they are demonstrating a lack of willingness to co-parent cooperatively at a minimum, and when the issue is as serious as blocking contact and communication, it can really look bad.

The second type of response, and probably the most common, is an angry rant that doesn't suggest any potential solution to the problem you raised. They'll go on and on about what a terrible parent you are and maybe even how it's so hard to make the calls happen because the kids don't even want to talk with you. Try to set your emotions aside for a moment. What they're saying about the kids not wanting to speak with you probably isn't true, but regardless, "their anger is your gold," as attorney Yoni Levoritz once told us. There's probably a lot a lawyer could do with a stack of communications from your ex claiming your kids don't want to talk with you, starting with a tangible demonstration of their refusal to follow court orders.

By far the least common response to your well-constructed strategic communication is the best outcome: they'll actually solve the problem. If that happens, it's time to celebrate. But keep your expectations in check: this is not likely.

Turning things around with your communication takes time and patience, and you may never get to a full solution this way. But it's worth a shot, and serves the additional purpose of giving you potentially priceless documentation.

Always keep in mind that you're probably not going to fix everything all at once. This is about incrementally making progress: to go from no contact with your kids to a little bit, and from a little contact to a little bit more. It's about slowly but consistently reversing the impact of what's happened and moving things in the other direction.

### General Guidelines

When you're communicating strategically with your ex, try to follow these guidelines as closely as you can:

- **Avoid "*I*," "*you*," "*me*," "*my*," etc.** Sometimes, these words are unavoidable, as in our example ("my" scheduled calls), but a toxic person will take them as confrontational. "*We*" and "*our*," on the other hand, suggest positive engagement and collaboration (remember, you're writing for that invisible audience!).

- **Make sure your universal agreement, or anchor, is truly universal**—something no reasonable person could have a problem with. It can be tempting to bake your proposed solution into this agreement ("I'm sure we can both agree that having the kids go to reunification therapy with me would be a good next step"). That one's probably not gonna work.
- **Don't suggest or offer opinions.** Anything that's your idea will likely be shot down. The idea is to invite their solution. Let them feel in charge, as if they still have all the power.

Strategic communication is such a huge topic and critical piece of the big picture of how you can navigate the hell that is co-parenting with an abusive ex, that we made it the subject of the first course in our flagship "From Fear to Fierce in Family Court" program. This course is called *Strategic Communication: How to Communicate with Your Ex Without Destroying Your Case or Losing Your Mind*, and you can learn more about it in our free webinar that is itself packed with useful tips, just one of the resources we put together as a supplement to this book, here:

In case you're not able to use this QR code, it links to https://BeenThereGotOut.com/Book2. We have useful resources on this page, including links to a lot of the interviews we've excerpted in this book.

Let's now look at a few other strategies you can try to influence your ex:

## Leverage Third Parties

Your ex might be impossible for you to work with, but sometimes they care deeply about being liked by others, especially those who know both of you in a co-parenting context; you may, at some point, have experienced your ex putting on a big act to win over those in your shared world. Now might be the time to put that dynamic to good use. If recommendations come from a third party, your ex might be more inclined to follow them. See if you can get that other person to deliver a recommendation that aligns with your wishes to do whatever it takes to get your kids what they need.

One of Chris' sons was having some struggles that he felt could be addressed in therapy, but he knew his ex would never agree. Since school attendance was being affected, he spoke with his son's counselor and very delicately explained that he and his ex, regrettably, struggled to make decisions cooperatively. The counselor agreed to reach out to Chris' ex directly with the idea of therapy, and like an on-time train, his ex presented the brilliant idea as if it were her own.

## Reverse Psychology

Your ex might be so predictably oppositional that you can use reverse psychology to get what you want. Sometimes, parents face a major decision that your custody agreement requires you to consult on and make together. If your ex is following court orders and involving you, but always deciding the opposite of what you think is best, reverse psychology just might work.

When Chris' other son was younger, he struggled with severe OCD, which is in the anxiety disorder family. Chris and his ex had tried lots of different therapeutic solutions throughout his childhood, none of which alleviated the symptoms. After the separation, their son's therapist suggested they consider powerful medication, not a decision to be taken lightly. Chris thought it was worth a try, but knew if he expressed his view, his ex would be against it.

So, the theme of his communication on the issue was, "Gee, I don't know…these drugs are serious stuff." It was a calculated risk, but his ex didn't disappoint with her invective-laden "I'm in charge!" responses. In the end, Chris' son got the medication, and it helped him greatly.

### You May Not Solve the Problem, But...

It's entirely possible that you won't be able to get anywhere working directly with your ex, but always keep in mind that actually fixing a problem may not be your only goal. Just documenting your attempts to work cooperatively can make you look great to any third party who gets involved in your case.

### Questions for Reflection

1. What influence might you have with your ex that you haven't fully considered? Think about what they care about most (reputation, public image, legal consequences, money, avoiding conflict with authorities), and how you might use this strategically.

2. Looking at your recent communications with your ex, which strategic communication mistakes have you been making? Are you using too many "I/you" statements,

getting defensive, offering your own solutions instead of inviting theirs, or showing emotion? What specific changes will you make in your next interaction to build better documentation while potentially influencing their behavior?

## CHAPTER 16

# STAYING STRONG & SEEING IT THROUGH

*"Love is the antidote for everything...love and security. If your child feels loved, secure, and safe, they will be fine."*

— Theresa Inman, Behavioral Analyst

### Self-Sabotaging

Sharing custody with an alienating ex is a marathon. The biggest reason people lose is that they become exhausted and give up before getting an outcome that they can live with, in or out of the legal system. No matter how strongly your child voices wanting nothing to do with you anymore, if you walk away, it will be perceived as you rejecting them. Studies by Dr. Amy Baker with adult alienated children revealed that they felt both hurt and angry when a targeted parent stopped trying to maintain the relationship.

Adult alienated children said that the targeted parent should not have believed them at the time because they were going through the motions of rejection, but they still did love them and did not want to lose the relationship.

We don't want you to sabotage your situation by making decisions out of frustration or fatigue that could harm you and make things worse for your kids.

## They Want Safety Again

When we're in the thick of things, it can feel hopeless. The reality, says alienation coach Charlie McCready, is that the majority of rejected parents do end up having relationships with their kids. Connections may change, depending on how badly the child's been affected, how we have been affected, and the length of time this has gone on. We'll probably discover that our child is different by the time they're re-engaging with us.

We parents don't permit ourselves to go through the healing process because we feel guilty spending time on ourselves. We don't realize there's a critical link between really wanting to help your kids and the need to help yourself, and you should be doing it for yourself anyway, because every rejected parent is worthy and deserves a good life. You've got to be healed enough so that you are not getting triggered anymore by your child, as only then can you have a heartfelt conversation where you are focused on them. When you're not, your kids will know.

When we get reactive, it can be as subtle as changing our tone of voice, facial expression, body language, or just going silent. Your nonverbal signals have to match what's coming out of your mouth. So even if you're saying the right things, your kid feels when it's disingenuous. Your child needs to feel safe with you again. Don't let the anger that has built up inside you all this time come gushing out.

If you do this, you're just going to push your kid away again, because they're going to think that you are still dwelling on the conflict with their other parent. If your kid brings up your ex, it may be because they want to have a normal relationship and be able to talk about their life, and they want that to be okay with you.

McCready says that our bodies are always releasing energy and that our hearts are sending out signals that our kids will pick up on. So when we're with them, we need to have two conversations in our heads.

- Am I one hundred percent focused on my kid and what they need from me (love and support)?
- What's going on within me? Am I doing everything in my power not to let whatever it is come between me and my child?

## Roots in Insecurity

"The majority of people who seem to end up with narcissists are empaths," says McCready, "and we're empaths because of the experiences that we had when we were younger... very often it's because we haven't been given the love and support that we deserved as children."

This lack of security in our youth may have undermined our confidence and self-worth, and made us conflict-avoidant people pleasers. What we now end up doing is trying to people-please our kids: walking on eggshells around them, terrified that we're not going to be able to rebuild that relationship. All of those childhood fears are swirled up and tied back to not feeling any sense of safety.

## Three Dead Ends

The more you can be a detective and try to remain curious about what your kid has to say and how they got here, the more focused your effort to strengthen the relationship can be. Some mistakes we may unconsciously make when dealing with kids who have turned against us include:

1. **Believing that life is fair.** Unfortunately, it's not. How it got to this point is not the issue; how to get your kid back is.

2. **Using guilt to show how much you've already invested in them.** There is no scoreboard for raising your children.
3. **Returning fire.** Your defensiveness towards your child distracts from their feelings. You don't have to tolerate abuse, but reciprocating doesn't win their heart back.

## You Can Learn

As the ever-inspirational parenting coach Mike Barsamian says, "Let's get that version of you back to the top." No matter how done you think you are, there is some part of you that is not ready to give up. After all, you have read this book!

Human beings are meaning-making machines who attach significance to everything. Sometimes you are just believing the wrong story and need to be reminded of how good you are. You deserve to live a happy, whole, connected life.

## Your Value

Alienation is a social epidemic. There are probably more abusive parents whose kids would never turn against them than there are wonderful, loving parents whose children do. No one ever imagines that the person you once loved would betray you so deeply by stealing your child's heart. And no, you didn't deserve this because "everything happens for a reason."

Fixating on decisions you could have made over the years is an enormous waste of time and energy. What's done is done.

Having a child reject you is not proof that you are unlovable. Sometimes our children are the least appropriate people to tell us what kinds of parents we are, most especially those brainwashed by a toxic co-parent. As Dr. Josh Coleman says, "Your value isn't for your child or anyone else to determine. Your value is part of your birthright, and you should guard it with your life." You are going to be dealing with ongoing pain and need to tend to yourself. This means taking care of your body by eating well, exercising, and getting enough sleep (easier said than done, we know!), and also by finding people who can sit with you in this ache.

As Katie Ripman, UK founder of the Single Mama Club, says, "None of us prepared for this, and it's not fair, and we really have to take the time to honor that... But is it going to define you and carve out the rest of your life?"

## Next Steps

We are constantly publishing interviews with experts on our YouTube channel and podcast. Just search *Been There Got Out…* we're very easy to find.

Our website at BeenThereGotOut.com has loads of resources, including our blog, designed to help people going through high-conflict divorces, the worst custody battles, and co-parenting hell.

Lastly, we have a page on our site dedicated to providing supplemental materials specifically for readers of this book, at https://BeenThereGotOut.com/Book2. This QR code will take you right there:

**"If there's ever anything you want to know more about, please don't hesitate to reach out to us!"**

—Lisa Johnson and Chris Barry

## ACKNOWLEDGEMENTS

Our clients are the reason we do what we do. Your stories of perseverance inspire us daily, and your challenges drive us to expand our knowledge and connections to resources. You pave the way for the others who follow. Thanks so much for trusting us with your lives.

More broadly, the same can be said about our wonderful social media community, especially on Instagram. Thank you for the engagement, ideas for content, and excellent quotes!

Thanks to countless caring experts, always way too many to mention, but those who inspired and/or are included in this book are attorneys: Ashish Joshi, Charlie Jamieson, Kevin Hoffkins, Arique Dross, Billie Tarascio, Yoni Levoritz, Stephanie T., Sean Valentine, Brian Pakpour, Evynne Fair, Leona Krasner, Nicolle Kopping-Pavars, Mia Poppe, and Maribeth Blessing;

Mental health professionals, psychologists, psychiatrists, researchers, social workers, and therapists: Dr. Amy Baker, Adam Barta, Theresa Inman, Steven G. Miller, Richard A. Warshak, Paul Fine, Dr. Alina Boie, Dr. Christopher Willard, Dr. David Marcus, Edel Lawlor, Jessica Anne Pressler, Dr. Jill Leibowitz, Dr. Josh Coleman, Dr. Kristin A. Roorbach, Lauren Barnett, Leslie Miller, Dr. Liz Stilwell, Dr. Mark Singer, Marnie Grundman, Nicholas Bala, Nicole Kristal, and Dr. Rebecca Vasquez;

Coaches Charlie McCready, Tosha Schore, Susie Pettit, Clarissa Constantine, Darlynn Childress, Jon McKenney, Kristen Darcy, and Mike Barsamian;

Assorted experts: AJ Gajjar, Tara Zacharzuk-Marciano, Dawn Brauer, Diana Canas, Judge Michael Haas, Judge Lynn Toler, Kelly Corrigan, Maarit (Blended Family Frappe), Tyra Juliette, Philly Yonta, and Women Aware, Kelly and Abigail White, and Melissa Lowry;

And to our guru, social worker, family lawyer, and founder of the High Conflict Institute, who graciously agreed to write the Foreword to this book, Bill Eddy, whose numerous books have helped save our clients' (and our own) lives.

Speaking of inspiring books, we relied heavily on research from the following three books:

- *Litigating Parental Alienation*...by Ashish Joshi (ABA, 2021)
- *Don't Alienate the Kids!*...by Bill Eddy (UCI Press, 2020)
- *Co-Parenting With a Toxic Ex*...by Dr. Amy J. L. Baker and Paul R. Fine (New Harbinger, 2014)

We also would like to thank everyone who has contributed to our interviews or hosted us, as well as our families, our amazing publishers Patrice Samara and Marva Allen at Wordeee, and Silvana, Marta, Adrienne, Kelly, and especially Davidsa and her family.

# ABOUT THE AUTHORS

## Lisa Johnson

Lisa Johnson is a Certified Domestic Violence Advocate, a trained crisis counselor, an educator, a professional writer, and a former high school English teacher. She represented herself (*pro se*) in family and appellate court through eight years and more than one hundred court appearances, which was a job unto itself.

Lisa received her B.A. from SUNY Albany, and Master's degree from the University of Bridgeport, and is a fellow of the Connecticut Writing Project. Lisa has written for *Mothering* Magazine, *Fit Pregnancy, Writer's Digest*, and other publications. She has been a guest on CNN and quoted in the *New York Times*.

## Chris Barry

Chris Barry is a Certified High-Conflict Divorce Coach who has also successfully represented himself post-judgment. Before launching BTGO with Lisa, he built another online business that attracted over 35,000 avid fans. His background is in software sales for several startups, one of which was acquired by Microsoft. Earlier, he was a Financial Advisor for a decade, and is fluent in personal financial issues.

Chris earned a B.S. in Marketing from Lehigh University and an MBA in Management Information Systems from Seton Hall University. He's an avid golfer and has an admittedly unhealthy lifelong love for the NFL's Miami Dolphins.

Lisa and Chris' first book, *Been There Got Out: Toxic Relationships, High-Conflict Divorce, and How to Stay Sane Under Insane Circumstances* (Wordeee, 2023), is a comprehensive overview of the divorce/custody process for people getting out of relationships with narcissists and other high-conflict personality types.

BTGO has published 300+ interviews with experts of all kinds on their YouTube channel, and their large, engaged following on Instagram is a rare exception to the toxicity that pervades social media. They have become a leading voice in their field and a go-to resource for practical, actionable advice worldwide.

Chris and Lisa have also been a romantic couple since 2015. But that's a story for another time.

www.ingramcontent.com/pod-product-compliance
Lightning Source LLC
LaVergne TN
LVHW012038070526
838202LV00056B/5530